W9-BAH-676

PAUL McCARTNEY

I Saw Him Standing There

JORIE B. GRACEN

BILLBOARD BOOKS
an imprint of Watson-Guptill Publications
New York

ACKNOWLEDGMENTS

I would like to express my special thanks to: Mindy Kolof for her suggestions and editing help; Bill King and the staff at *Beatlefan* magazine for their excellent input and resources; my agents, Andrea Brown and Laura Rennert, who shared the same vision; Lynette Stark, who pointed me in the right direction; Bob Nirkind, Alison Hagge, and Jay Anning at Billboard Books for a brilliant collaboration; my brother, Dr. Todd L. Gracen, for his guidance; and my friends who convinced me to do this book—Debbra Glienke, Sandy Lopez, Cris Noll, Linda Reig, Wilma Skinner, Laura Waskin, Pam Dupre, Barry King, and John and Tina Carlson.

Special thanks to: Mike Oltersdorf, Jennifer DeBernardis, Sue Ullenberg, Jean Catharell, Leslie King, Richard Porter, Philippe Colinge, Valerie Despré, Andrew Brooks, Jude Montoya, Sheryl Shorts, and Colin Barratt; and Lynn Harvey and Cathy Munro of the Macca-list.

This book is dedicated to my parents, Sidney and Lillian Gracen, who gave their love, support, and encouragement. And to Paul and Linda McCartney, who were my inspiration.

Title page:

On a cold, rainy night in Milwaukee, Paul shows disbelief at the uncooperative weather. June 2, 1993, Milwaukee County Stadium, Milwaukee, Wisconsin.

Facing page photos (from top):

McCartney croons "Venus and Mars are all right tonight" from the show's opening number. Around his neck are a sculptured pair of bird wings and a "Wings at the Speed of Sound" medallion. June 21, 1976, Forum, Inglewood, California.

One of the actual picks used by Paul during the late 1970s.

Paul concentrates on bass and smiles at the crowd during "Coming Up" at Earls Court, September 14, 1993, London, England.

One of three sold-out shows in Chicago. Paul rotates high above the audience on an elevated platform singing, "Round and round. . . ." The song was an audience favorite. "The Fool on the Hill," December 4, 1989, Rosemont Horizon, Rosemont, Illinois.

A LIPA guest laminate, which was given to a limited number of individuals who paid $1,000 for a charity ticket that provided backstage access, dinner, T-shirt, program, a McCartney sound check, and seats for the show. Proceeds went toward the building fund of McCartney's "Fame School" in Liverpool: the Liverpool Institute for Performing Arts. April 17, 1993, Anaheim Stadium, Anaheim, California.

HMV Music Store on Oxford Street welcomes Paul at a record signing, his first U.K. record signing in thirty years. October 16, 1997, London, England.

Copyright © 2000 by Jorie B. Gracen
First published in 2000 by Billboard Books
an imprint of Watson-Guptill Publications
a division of BPI Communications, Inc.
770 Broadway, New York, NY 10003
www.watsonguptill.com

Library of Congress Cataloging-in-Publication Data
Gracen, Jorie B.
   Paul McCartney : I saw him standing there / by Jorie B. Gracen.
      p.   cm.
   ISBN 0-8230-8372-1
   1. McCartney, Paul—Journeys. 2. Rock musicians—England—Biography. I. Title: I saw him standing there. II. Title

ML410.M115 G73 2000
782.42166'092—dc21
[B]
                                    00-039244

Manufactured in China
First printing, 2000
1 2 3 4 5 6 7 8 9 / 08 07 06 05 04 03 02 01 00

Senior Acquisitions Editor: Bob Nirkind
Associate Editor: Alison Hagge
Cover and interior design: Jay Anning, Thumb Print

The principal typefaces used in the composition of this book were 10 point Weidemann Book and 48 point Ariston Bold.

Contents

WINGS

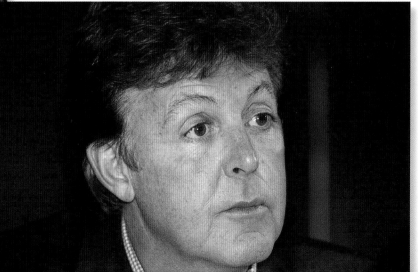

Foreword

I DON'T KNOW HOW YOUR MEMORY WORKS, but mine is rather like an internal multimedia scrapbook. Pick a subject and, in my head, the images and sounds unfold, taking me back to a place, a time, an unforgettable experience. A feeling.

Real scrapbooks, photo albums, home movies, and videos can create this effect as well, helping to unleash these memories. Though memories are often more inclusive than the images in these record-keeping formats, at least with scrapbooks and photo albums you can share the look back with someone else and recapture some of the feeling you had when it all happened.

For me and for anyone else who has been to a Paul McCartney concert over the years, Jorie Gracen's photos provide exactly that experience, setting the memories loose. Her own skillful still images, capturing McCartney onstage, set off the thousands of moving and morphing mental images I've retained from the nearly two dozen times I've seen him perform since 1976.

Ah, yes, the Bicentennial year. It seemed like we'd been waiting forever for McCartney to tour, though it was just a few months shy of ten years since he and the Beatles had given their farewell concert in San Francisco. A year and a half earlier some friends and I had spent a long, cold night sharing two thin blankets on the concrete sidewalk outside Atlanta's Omni as we waited for tickets for George Harrison's Atlanta shows to go on sale. A sort of bonding took place among the mostly college-age crowd that night. And the next morning, as one bedraggled young man was about to go through the gates to buy his tickets, he turned to the folks behind him and shouted, "I want to see all of you back right here in the middle line when Paul McCartney comes!"

Chances are, he did. But when my wife, brother, and I camped out to buy tickets for the Wings over America show at The Omni in the spring of '76, we came much better prepared, complete with sleeping bags and a cooler of food and drink.

When I really felt the shared experience, however, was the evening of the first Atlanta show, when we were all standing outside the arena while Wings did their sound check inside. I looked out over the thousands of fans and beheld a virtual sea of blue jeans. A generational thing, you might say.

Flash forward about three and one-half hours and another of the time-freezing images I still have of that visually dazzling, well-paced, thoroughly enjoyable show—"a study in controlled flash," *Time* magazine called it—is Macca, his '70s shag haircut now soaked with sweat, holding his bass guitar aloft at the end and promising, "See ya next time!" as he left the stage.

Two years later I added a sideline to my work as a newspaper rock critic by starting *Beatlefan* magazine, and was lucky to have access to lots of pictures from the '76 tour—most notably the shots from one of our contributing editors, which stood out from all the others. They were Jorie Gracen's.

Four years later . . . McCartney's Japanese pot bust had put the kibosh on his next planned Wings tour. And then we lost John Lennon to a lunatic assassin at the end of that year. I wasn't sure there'd really be a next time.

Finally, though, nine years later, my brother and I were on the floor of New York's Madison Square Garden in December 1989, excitedly awaiting the arrival onstage of Paul, Linda, and their new, nameless band. During the next eight months I would see better, tighter performances than the one at the Garden that night, but in retrospect none can match that first concert for sheer excitement.

Again, the images flow . . . McCartney and sideman Hamish Stuart sliding across the stage on their knees, ending up at the feet of guitarist Robbie McIntosh during his solo on "We Got

◀ McCartney grins at the howling audience, which has just witnessed the spectacular pyrotechnics during "Live and Let Die." Unsuspecting concertgoers were jolted out of their seats as bombs exploded, strobes flickered, and lasers bombarded the stadium. Paul stands amused at his piano, not yet visible to the audience because of the rising smoke. June 1, 1976, Chicago Stadium, Chicago, Illinois.

Married" . . . McCartney's face beaming during the extended "Sgt. Pepper's Lonely Hearts Club Band" . . . the explosive staging of the eternally popular "Live and Let Die" . . . the house lights going up to reveal the crowd singing and dancing along as one during a rip-roaring "Can't Buy Me Love" . . . the lighters blazing all over the hall during "Let It Be" . . . Macca and his two fellow guitarists pushing and shoving each other like kids in a garage band during the climactic guitar duel of "The End."

Beatlefan gave that 1989–90 McCartney tour probably the most extensive coverage any rock tour has ever received, and one of the primary features of that coverage was the photography of Jorie Gracen, which combined the warmth of a fan with the technical proficiency of a professional. I think Jorie's shots from London's Wembley Arena (where I also saw Paul twice on that tour) are among her best work. We felt a shared pride when one of Jorie's shots, which we had run, later was picked by Paul and Linda for inclusion in the booklet released with the tour's live album.

By the '90s many of McCartney's fans were in a much better position, financially and professionally, to follow a tour than they had been in '76, and so was born what we dubbed the "Fans on the Run," those of us not satisfied with merely seeing McCartney's stop in our own town. The process had evolved a bit—no more camping out, as a telephone speed dial became the ticket buyer's best friend—but the excitement level seemed not to have changed with age. And now I could experience it all through fresh eyes—those of my son.

The New World Tour of 1993 may not have created quite the buzz among the media and general populace that the '90 "comeback" tour did, but while the gee-whiz factor had lessened,

"Figure of Eight," Chicago style, December 5, 1989, Rosemont Horizon, Rosemont, Illinois. The crew of *48 Hours* videotaped all three concerts in Chicago and documented the McCartneys's stay there.

its staging was more sophisticated than ever thanks to the use of live video screens, and its musical performances were tighter and harder rocking.

And, for fans, it was full of more memorable moments—and images . . . McCartney and McIntosh out over the crowd in a cherry picker during "Let Me Roll It" (a rare nod to the Wings days) . . . the fireworks during "Live and Let Die" . . . the entire band out over the crowd in the cherry picker during the encore.

That tour also provided the single most spine-tingling McCartney tour moment I've experienced when, during "Yesterday," the Liberty Bowl in Memphis became ablaze with lighters held high in tribute and the crowd started cheering midsong. That's one mental image that still raises the hairs on my neck! *Beatlefan* again provided blanket coverage of the entire tour and, again, Jorie's photos were a highlight.

As I write this, Paul McCartney has returned to the stage of Liverpool's Cavern Club, with still another new band, and there's speculation that another tour might be in the offing. But even if he never tours again, Sir Paul has already provided us with a lifetime of memories to go with all those fantastic tunes. And many of them are concert memories. Though his greatest achievements might have occurred in the recording studio, when he's really enjoying himself onstage Paul McCartney is as fine a showman as rock has produced. And a splendid time is guaranteed for all.

Now we can relive those splendid times, thanks to Jorie Gracen and her camera.

—BILL KING, PUBLISHER, *BEATLEFAN* MAGAZINE

Introduction

IFIRST MET PAUL AND LINDA backstage at their last U.S. concert on the 1976 Wings over America World Tour. My career as a photojournalist was still in the making when my school paper assigned me to cover that historic tour. Celebrity assignments were quickly passed over by seasoned staff photographers because the veterans didn't want to deal with high-profile figures. Egos had to be stroked, polished, and patted on the back to get those one-of-a-kind photos. I rose to the challenge and photographing celebrities soon became a passion, with my photos appearing in major magazines.

Paul and Linda were a rare breed—down-to-earth in many respects, but very much in tune with the world and how they were perceived by the public. My first meeting with Paul was brief and I admit it was more of a fan meeting her idol than a student photographer getting a prized photo. Pressed for time, Paul tried his best to sign an autograph, but he was ushered into a limo by his staff and so he consoled me with a quick thumbs-up and a wave.

Our paths crossed again in 1978 when I flew to London on vacation and unexpectedly ran into Paul and Linda at Abbey Road Studios. The couple stopped to pose for photos without hesitation—something I greatly admired about them. Paul playfully pushed his nose up against my camera lens and began making silly faces, knowing that he was too close to photograph. Linda pulled him back to get a proper photo. Minutes later they were in the studio recording "Rockestra" from the *Back to the Egg* album.

Toward the beginning of the 1989–90 Paul McCartney World Tour, I was assigned to photograph McCartney for various publications. As a member of the working press my access was limited; however, during the course of the ten-month tour I acquired a vast collection of photos, which I decided to present to Paul as a thank you for allowing me to take his photo.

That opportunity came on July 29, 1990, at the last show of the world tour, which just happened to be in my hometown of Chicago. Backstage, as the famous couple posed for photos, I handed Paul my book. Ten days later I received a call from his London office asking permission to use one of the photographs on Paul's new album, *Tripping the Live Fantastic.* Out of thousands of photos taken by McCartney's tour photographers, Paul and Linda had found something unique about my photo that no other photographer had captured.

The album was released a few months later and I received an invitation to join Paul and Linda at a private London party to celebrate the official end of the world tour and the new album. When the couple arrived, they greeted me as if I were an old friend. I said to Paul, "I'm the one

▲ Paul and Linda pose for photos outside Abbey Road Studios, St. John's Wood, London, England, October 3, 1978, where they recorded "Rockestra" from the *Back to the Egg* album. Paul stuck his face right up against my camera lens and made silly faces, knowing he was too close to take photos.

◀ The invitation to the End of the World Tour Party at the Boardwalk Restaurant in the Soho section of London, England. Guests included his employees, tour crew, his daughters Mary and Stella, plus band members Robbie, Hamish, and Wix. December 12, 1990.

who took the photo on your album." He kiddingly asked, "Which one?" "This one!" I exclaimed, trying to imitate the pose. "No, I think it was more like this," he replied with a squint, checking my posture for accuracy. Then he assumed the position that was unmistakably a re-creation of the photo. I told him how much I appreciated the opportunity to have my photo on his album and he said, "I saw thousands of photos and yours was one of the best. Brilliant photo! Right, Linder?" He playfully nudged her with his elbow as she responded with a smile, "Yeah, great photo!" It was quite a compliment coming from a legendary rock star and a world-famous photographer.

Later I seized the moment and asked Paul if I could take a photo *with* him. "Well, let's get one done then!" he shouted, lifting me off the floor with one arm wrapped around my waist. I dangled like a doll, struggling to plant one foot on the ground, until he released his grip and we posed. In less time than it took to say "The Cute Beatle," McCartney was off terrorizing another fan with a similar request.

The uncropped photo that graces the inside booklet of *Tripping the Live Fantastic.* Linda McCartney was cropped from the album photo to fit the format. Paul makes his final leap at the end of "Golden Slumbers/ Carry That Weight/The End." February 14, 1990, Market Square Arena, Indianapolis, Indiana.

In 1993 I was given assignments to photograph McCartney during the New World Tour. Access was more limited due to fewer shows in large venues and McCartney's lack of desire to meet the press. The constant and redundant questions from reporters had finally irritated even the affable Paul, who subsequently chose to be more selective at his press events.

I saw him backstage at the Earth Day Concert at the Hollywood Bowl and surprisingly I was the only one who recognized him when he entered the press tent. He was dressed much like a roadie, wearing sunglasses and denim. Paul smiled as I took his photo, amused that nobody else was paying attention to him. My barrage of camera flashes alerted the curious, nonchalant members of the media, who upon discovering his presence said, "Oh Paul, we're not ready for you." His quick reply was: "Too BAD!" That was enough to encourage a volley of questions and mass hysteria to get video cameras rolling. He took it all in stride and even managed to keep one step ahead of the press horde that ran, screaming like a group of twelve-year-olds, after him—nearly running this photographer over in the melee— at the conclusion of the press conference.

Paul and Linda came back to Chicago in 1994 to debut Linda's new line of frozen vegetarian foods, and again in 1995, for the release of her cookbook, *Linda's Kitchen* (Little, Brown). At the book party Linda grabbed my arm and said, "I'm so glad to see you again!" She was full of enthusiasm—as was Paul, who shook my hand. Then we conversed about subjects ranging from recipes to his radio show, *Oobu Joobu.*

Abbey Road Studios

My favorite photo of Paul came about in May of 1997 when McCartney was recording *Standing Stone* (1997) at Abbey Road Studios. He drove up in a blue Mercedes and gave me the okay sign, promising something wonderful for my camera. As he walked from the car, he chatted with fans until he reached the steps leading up to the studio doors. After walking up the first two steps, McCartney paused, turned around to face me, and said, looking directly into my camera, "See, I'm posing on the steps of Abbey Road!" With a *click* I captured the rock legend—standing there—on the historic steps of Abbey Road Studios, with the famous sign above his head.

The last time I saw Linda was in New York, at the November 1997 Carnegie Hall performance of Paul's second classical composition, "Standing Stone." We had connected a month earlier at London's Royal Albert Hall for the world premiere of the piece, where she acknowledged me with a wave, looking quite stylish in her short hair and designer suit fashioned by daughter Stella.

▲ Paul poses for the author on the historic steps of Abbey Road Studios, where the Beatles recorded most of their albums. May 2, 1997, London, England, *Standing Stone* recording sessions.

▼ "I love YOU!" shouts Paul, pointing to Linda, who was cheering him on in the audience. Paul takes flowers offered by admirers and six curtain calls. "Standing Stone" premiere, Royal Albert Hall, London, England, October 14, 1997.

When Linda died from breast cancer in April 1998, it was a devastating loss to the world. She fought vehemently for animal rights, supported her husband musically onstage in spite of ridicule, produced a popular line of frozen vegetarian foods, published successful books on photography and cooking, raised four talented children, and might have accomplished much more had she lived. How blessed I was to have known her and I'll always be grateful that she recognized my work as a photographer.

With this book I've attempted to faithfully capture the most memorable moments of Paul McCartney on tour as well as photos from the nontouring years. My special thanks to the many fans who shared their loving stories about meeting Paul and Linda. Although there will never be another tour with both McCartneys onstage, the future holds a promise that Paul will tour again. This collection of photos and stories preserves the legacy of a time when, together, the McCartneys conquered the world with their gift of love and music.

—JORIE B. GRACEN

1972–1973 CONCERT DATES

1972 UK February 9: Nottingham University, Nottingham, England • February 10: York University, York, England • February 11: Hull University, Hull, England • February 13: Newcastle-upon-Tyne University, Newcastle-upon-Tyne, England • February 14: Lancaster University, Lancaster, England • February 16: Leeds Town Hall, Leeds, England • February 17: Sheffield University, Sheffield, England • February 18: Manchester University, Manchester, England • February 21: Birmingham University, Birmingham, England • February 22: Swansea University, Swansea, Wales • February 23: Oxford University, Oxford, England **1972 EUROPE** July 9: Centre Culturel, Chateauvallon, France • July 12: Théâtre Antique, Antibes Juan-les-Pins, France • July 13: Théâtre Antique, Arles, France • July 16: Olympia Theatre, Paris, France (two shows) • July 18: Circus-Krone-Bau, Munich, Germany • July 19: Offenbach-Halle, Frankfurt, Germany • July 21: Kongresshaus, Zurich, Switzerland • July 22: Switzerland Pavilion, Montreux, Switzerland • August 1: K. B. Hallen, Copenhagen, Denmark • August 4: Messuhalli, Helsinki, Finland • August 5: Kupittaan Urheiluhalli, Turku, Finland • August 7: Kungliga Hallen, Stockholm, Sweden • August 8: Idretshalle, Örebro, Sweden • August 9: Njaardhallen, Oslo, Norway • August 10: Scandinavium Hall, Göteborg, Sweden • August 11: Olympean, Lund, Sweden • August 12: Fyns Forum, Odense, Denmark • August 14: Vejlby Risskov Hallen, Århus, Denmark • August 16: Rhinehalle, Düsseldorf, Germany • August 17: Doelen, Rotterdam, The Netherlands • August 19: Evenementenhal, Groningen, The Netherlands • August 20: Concertgebouw, Amsterdam, The Netherlands • August 21: Congresgebouw, The Hague, The Netherlands • August 22: Cine Roma, Antwerp, Belgium • August 24: Deutschlandhalle, Berlin, Germany **1973 UK** May 11: Hippodrome, Bristol, England • May 12: New Theatre, Oxford, England • May 13: Capitol, Cardiff, Wales • May 15: Winter Gardens, Bournemouth, England • May 16, 17: Hard Rock, Manchester, England • May 18: The Empire Theatre, Liverpool, England • May 19: Leeds University, Leeds, England • May 21: Guildhall, Preston, England • May 22, 23: Odeon, Edinburgh, Scotland • May 24: Green Playhouse, Glasgow, Scotland • May 25, 26, 27: Odeon Hammersmith, Hammersmith, England • July 4: City Hall, Sheffield, England • July 6: Odeon Cinema, Birmingham, England • July 9: Odeon Cinema, Leicester, England • July 10: City Hall, Newcastle-upon-Tyne, England

1975 UK September 6: Elstree Film Studios (rehearsal), London, England • September 9: Gaumont Cinema, Southampton, England • September 10: Hippodrome Cinema, Bristol, England • September 11: Capitol Cinema, Cardiff, Wales • September 12: Free Trade Hall, Manchester, England • September 13: Hippodrome, Birmingham, England • September 15: Empire Theatre, Liverpool, England • September 16: City Hall, Newcastle-upon-Tyne, England • September 17, 18: Odeon Hammersmith, Hammersmith, England • September 20: Usher Hall, Edinburgh, Scotland • September 21: Apollo Theatre, Glasgow, Scotland • September 22: Capitol Cinema, Aberdeen, Scotland • September 23: Caird Hall, Dundee, Scotland

1975 WINGS OVER AUSTRALIA November 1: Entertainment Centre, Perth, Australia • November 4, 5: Apollo Stadium, Adelaide, Australia • November 7, 8: Hordern Pavilion, Sydney, Australia • November 10, 11: Festival Hall, Brisbane, Australia • November 13, 14: Myer Music Bowl, Melbourne, Australia **1976 WINGS OVER EUROPE** March 20, 21: Falkoner Theatre, Copenhagen, Denmark • March 23: Deutschlandhalle, Berlin, Germany • March 25: Ahoy Sportpaleis, Rotterdam, The Netherlands • March 26: Pavilion, Paris, France

1976 WINGS OVER AMERICA USA/CANADA May 3: Tarrant County Convention Hall, Fort Worth, Texas • May 4: The Summit, Houston, Texas • May 7, 8: Olympia Stadium, Detroit, Michigan • May 9: Maple Leaf Gardens, Toronto, Canada • May 10: Richfield Coliseum, Cleveland, Ohio •

May 12, 14: Spectrum, Philadelphia, Pennsylvania •
May 15, 16: Capitol Centre, Largo, Maryland • May 18, 19: The
Omni, Atlanta, Georgia • May 21: Nassau Coliseum, Uniondale,
New York • May 22: Boston Garden, Boston, Massachusetts • May
24, 25: Madison Square Garden, New York, New York • May 27:
Riverfront Coliseum, Cincinnati, Ohio • May 29: Kemper Arena,
Kansas City, Missouri • May 31 and June 1, 2: Chicago Stadium,
Chicago, Illinois • June 4: Civic Center, St. Paul, Minnesota • June 7:
McNichols Arena, Denver, Colorado • June 10: Kingdome, Seattle,
Washington • June 13, 14: Cow Palace, San Francisco, California • June 16:
Sports Arena, San Diego, California • June 18: Community Center,
Tucson, Arizona • June 21, 22, 23: Forum, Inglewood,
California   1976 WINGS OVER EUROPE   September
19: Stadthalle, Vienna, Austria • September
21: Dom Sportova Hall, Zagreb,
Yugoslavia • September 25: Piazza San
Marco, Venice, Italy • September 27:
Olympiahalle, Munich, Germany
 1976 WINGS UK TOUR   October 19, 20, 21:
Empire Pool, Wembley Park, England

▲ Top billing at Olympia Stadium, home of the Detroit Red Wings, where for two nights it was home to Paul McCartney and Wings. May 7 and 8, 1976, Detroit, Michigan.

▶ Paul grins from ear to ear, trying to control himself from laughing because the boyfriend of a fan in the front row is trying desperately to get his date's attention. It's all in vain because she only has eyes for Paul. McCartney taunts her even more with the Macca-hop-strut-march during "Silly Love Songs." June 2, 1976, Chicago Stadium, Chicago, Illinois.

1975–1976 Wings over the World Tour

ON SEPTEMBER 13, 1971, Paul and Linda officially named their newly formed band "Wings." It was just more than a year since the official breakup of the Beatles and Paul was well on his way as a solo artist. He released two albums, *McCartney* (1970) and *Ram* (1971), with the help of his wife, Linda, and session drummer Denny Seiwell (*Ram*). Ex–Moody Blues guitarist Denny Laine and guitarist Henry McCullough (formerly of the Grease Band) joined the group, and on December 7 Wings's first album, *Wildlife,* was released. Small tours of the United Kingdom and Europe followed in early 1972, as McCartney introduced his new band to the world.

Critics were less than kind. One even referred to the newly formed Wings as McCartney's "hangover" from the Beatles. Undaunted, McCartney and his band produced five Wings albums—all certified gold—in the years leading up to the 1975–76 world tour, despite the fact that the band went through many personnel changes.

Band on the Run, McCartney's most critically acclaimed post-Beatles effort with Wings, was released on December 5, 1973. At that time Wings consisted of three members: Paul, Linda, and Denny Laine. Henry McCullough and Denny Seiwell quit just before the recording sessions in Lagos, Nigeria, leaving Paul no choice but to record with the two remaining members. *Band on the Run* was an unexpected success, sparking McCartney's vision that Wings could work together as a creative unit with each member contributing to the musical identity of the group. It was an ambitious undertaking—but necessary for McCartney, who was determined to establish Wings as a first-rate rock-and-roll band. Two years later he transformed the disjointed group into a precision touring band capable of unleashing its own musical force.

As the fall of 1975 approached, Wings had a fresh lineup and a major world tour scheduled to start in Britain and Australia, followed by Europe and the United States. Wings personnel included: Paul McCartney (bass, guitar, piano, keyboards, vocals); Denny Laine (guitar, vocals, percussion, piano), a Wings member since 1971; Jimmy McCulloch (lead guitar, vocals), formerly of Thunderclap Newman and Stone the Crows, who joined Wings in 1974 and debuted on "Junior's Farm"; Joe English (drummer), formerly of the Jam Factory, who was asked to work on the *Venus and Mars* album in 1975; Linda McCartney (keyboards, vocals, and tambourine); Howie Casey (tenor sax), a Liverpudlian (Liverpool native) like McCartney, who had formed his own group in 1958 called Howie Casey and the Seniors; Steve Howard Jr. (trumpet, flügelhorn), who played trumpet during the *Venus and Mars* sessions in New Orleans; Thaddeus Richard (sax, flute), formerly of the Hip-Huggers and Reality, who recorded with Wings during the Nashville sessions; Tony Dorsey (trombone), a Nashville session musician and musical arranger who worked on *Venus and Mars.*

In the traditional style of live rock 'n' roll, this band added a harder edge, improving upon the recorded versions of the songs. Not since the Beatles had Paul played with a band that was so disciplined and adept at performing his most successful songs.

On March 23, 1976, Wings released a new album called *Wings at the Speed of Sound* that became a best-seller during the Wings over America Tour. It received gold record certification by R.I.A.A. (Recording Industry Association of America) for selling 500,000 units upon release, and quickly went platinum, with sales of more than one million. The hit single "Silly Love Songs" went to number one on the U.S. charts (according to *Billboard* magazine) on May 22. The tour, which had been scheduled to start on April 8 in the United States, was rescheduled for May and June when lead guitarist Jimmy McCulloch slipped in a Paris bathroom on March 26 and fractured his left finger. Tickets purchased months earlier reflected the original date of the show

Moody lighting surrounds Paul as he plays "Yesterday," which he introduced by saying, "See if you remember this tune. . . ." Following the song he tripped over a red carnation I threw on stage. After picking up the offending flower, he waved it in my direction and grinned. June 1, 1976, Chicago Stadium, Chicago, Illinois.

(i.e., the May 5, 1976, Chicago Stadium show was rescheduled for June 2, 1976).

By the time McCartney came to America with Wings in May of 1976 it had been almost a decade since the Beatles's last concert (August 29, 1966, at San Francisco's Candlestick Park). The twenty-plus member entourage traveled on a private jet (BAC 1011, leased from Braniff) and had "home bases" in Dallas, New York, Chicago, and Los Angeles. The McCartneys—a tight-knit family—traveled with their three young children: Stella, 4, Mary, 6, and Heather, 13. Also traveling with them were their nanny, Rose, and a tutor for Heather. McCartney was accompanied by band members, security guards, recording engineers, publicists, and other essential personnel that included Robert Ellis, a tour photographer, cartoonist Humphrey Ocean, who would "draw" the tour highlights for a book, and Paul's manager, Brian Brolly.

The 1975–76 Wings over the World Tour played in ten countries during the course of fourteen months—for a total of sixty-five concerts before two million people. The Wings over America Tour (the U.S. leg of the tour) played thirty-one shows in twenty-one cities, with an estimated audience of 600,000. A record-breaking attendance of 67,100 (1,100 more than the fixed seating) for an indoor performance was set at Seattle's Kingdome. Ticket sales for the world tour grossed between five and eight million dollars, with each ticket costing between $7.50 and $9.50 and with scalpers snaring $125 for the first five rows. The Philadelphia show grossed $336,000, making it one of the largest box office receipts in rock history for that time.

Months later, on December 10, *Wings over America,* a live triple album recorded during the U.S. tour, went to number one on the American charts. It was the first triple album by a band ever to reach number one in the United States.

McCartney chose only five Beatles songs in his set list of thirty numbers: "Lady Madonna," "Long and Winding Road," "I've Just Seen a Face," "Blackbird," and "Yesterday." The two-hour, fifteen-minute show also featured: "Venus and Mars," "Rock Show," "Jet," "Let Me Roll It," "Spirits of Ancient Egypt," "Medicine Jar," "Maybe I'm Amazed," "Call Me Back Again," "Live and Let Die," an acoustic set of "Picasso's Last Words," "Richard Cory," and "Bluebird." The show continued with: "You Gave Me the Answer," "Magneto and Titanium Man," "Go Now" (Los Angeles only), "My Love," "Listen to What the Man Said," "Let 'Em In," "Time to Hide," "Silly Love Songs," "Beware My Love," "Letting Go," "Band on the Run," and encores of "Hi Hi Hi," and "Soily." Most of the songs were from the post-Beatles albums *Red Rose Speedway* (1973), *Band on the Run, Venus and Mars, Wings at the Speed of Sound,* and *McCartney.*

The concert began with the "Venus and Mars/Rock Show" medley as tiny bubbles slowly descended from the ceiling. Billowing clouds of heavy fog enveloped the performers, while colored spotlights defined their positions onstage. "Red lights, green lights . . ." shone right on cue as Paul, who was covered in darkness, sang the words and then emerged dramatically in a spotlight—to screams of rapture from female fans. This was first time the ex-Beatle appeared live onstage since his departure from the group and the members of the audience were on their feet, behaving as if they were at a Beatles concert.

People were in awe of McCartney. A fusillade of camera flashes lit up the stadium walls in a continuous sea of flickering lights. People rushed the stage, but Paul maintained control with his gregarious charm, baiting the audience with his occasional stage banter: "ALRIGHT? Aaall, right!

▲ "We're going to have a little sit down with our acoustic guitars," says Paul who takes his seat with the other band members for the next song, "Richard Cory," which was sung by Denny Laine. June 1, 1976, Chicago Stadium, Chicago, Illinois.

◄ "Rock Show," California style. In the crowd were celebrities, including Mickey Dolenz, Cher, Elton John, Jack Nicholson, and Ringo Starr. A marching band paraded around the stadium prior to the show entertaining concertgoers who waited at a red carpet for stars to arrive. June 21, 1976, Forum, Inglewood, California.

▲ Ringo Starr surprises his former band mate onstage after the last song with a bouquet of flowers. The audience went crazy—expecting a performance from the ex-Beatles, which didn't happen. Paul and Ringo acknowledge the standing ovation and thunderous applause. It was the first time both appeared onstage together since the breakup of the Beatles. June 21, 1976, Forum, Inglewood, California.

▶ A touching moment as Paul and Ringo hug. Backstage they celebrate their reunion with a party that lasts well into the night. June 21, 1976, Forum, Inglewood, California.

Do you fancy a bit of rock 'n' roll?" McCartney playfully introduced "Yesterday," saying "I think you'll remember this one . . ." and playing the familiar opening chords as he sang "Chicago, Chicago . . ." (in Chicago). Other cities had similar "appropriate" fake beginnings to McCartney's most famous song.

At many of the concerts McCartney wore black satin trousers with a slight bell at the bottom and a black or white T-shirt covered by a long-sleeved black knitted hip-length jacket. Colored rhinestones adorned the shoulders of the jacket, complementing the pink satin lapels. Linda wore a formfitting black dress with white feather trim on the shoulders. Tour outfits varied from show to show, with Paul and Linda sometimes wearing matching waist-length satin black-and-white jackets with "X" and "O" decorations, symbols from the *Venus and Mars* album. Paul wore a short blue-and-white robe during his Australian concerts, which preceded the American tour.

The performance was divided into three parts: an opening set that rocked with "Rock Show," "Jet," "Lady Madonna," and "Live and Let Die"; a sit-down acoustic set featuring the emotional highlight of the show, "Yesterday"; and a closing set containing some of Wings's biggest hits, "My Love," "Silly Love Songs," "Hi Hi Hi," and "Band on the Run."

Dazzling stage effects included green lasers, pyrotechnics, and flickering strobe lights. "Live and Let Die," an audience favorite, used multiple flash pots that exploded during the song, giving unsuspecting fans a heart-stopping jolt. Flashing strobe lights and lasers bombarded the stage, creating a slow-motion effect intensified by the band's wild onstage antics of running and jumping. "Live and Let Die," a surefire crowd pleaser, was also performed on later tours.

"Magneto and Titanium Man" had a colorful backdrop, created by pop artist David Hockney, that depicted the Marvel comic-strip characters. Colored spotlights of red and yellow painted the performers, adding a playful atmosphere to the song.

"You Gave Me the Answer" was brought alive by hundreds of flashing white bulbs lining the multilevel stage. While Paul crooned in his best Rudy Vallee voice the syncopated lights moved in different directions, imitating a grandiose stage from a Fred Astaire movie.

A film backdrop shown during "Band on the Run" featured photographer Clive Arrowsmith's album-cover photo session, filmed by director Barry Chattington. Appearing in the film with Paul, Linda, and Denny were an assortment of characters, including actors James Coburn and Christopher Lee, who posed in prison outfits as they simulated a jailbreak.

"Soily," the final encore, deployed lasers projected in a fanlike pattern swirling beneath clouds of smoke. The pulsating green beams moved rhythmically above the audience, creating an eerie circling effect—which was dramatically enhanced by the haunting echoes of squealing keyboards.

One of the most memorable moments of the tour was a surprise appearance by Ringo Starr, who joined his former band mate onstage June 21 at the Forum in Inglewood, California. McCartney had just finished "Soily" and was taking his bows when a sunglassed Ringo Starr bounded onto the stage with a bouquet of flowers, grabbed Paul's bass, and struck a pose. The crowd went crazy when Paul and Ringo hugged, then turned to the audience, hands outstretched, acknowledging the thunderous applause. It was the first time in ten years the two ex-Beatles had stood together on the same stage. Although this wasn't the Beatles reunion fans had hoped for, it later became the catalyst that fueled future reunion rumors.

When the world tour culminated in London on October 21, 1976, it had achieved what McCartney had envisioned—Wings was a full-fledged rock-and-roll band worthy of the musical respect attributed to his former band, the Beatles. McCartney emerged triumphantly in the midst of criticism that claimed his "new" band would never be as good as his "old" one. From that point on he never looked back.

Back in 1975 I decided go to England. During my stay I took in the sights and smells of the Beatles's London, accompanied by a cheery Australian roommate, who taunted me with a "special surprise" during my entire stay. But it wasn't until the last day in town that my roomie finally produced that surprise: He had prepared a most special moment and even a speech for the occasion.

"Giry," he said, clearing his throat in a way only Australians can. "I know 'ow much you love the Beytels, and even though I'm more of a Dive Clark Five man moyself, it really 'as been fun followin' you 'round ray-cordin' studio parkin' lots and gettin' yelled at by that beeg guy owtside of George 'arrison's caysel. En sow . . . ," he continued, reaching with a flourish inside his jacket pocket, "I got us theese. Jest a leetel somethin' to selly-brite your last noit in England." He thrust an envelope into my hand.

I wondered what it could be. An extension to my visitor's visa? A hand-written apology from Allan Williams (the Beatles's first manager)? My cohort in madness began grinning nervously. Did this mean we were now engaged or something? I'd heard stories about randy Australians on the pounce in Britain, but my sense of propriety relaxed as I peeked inside and removed two shiny new concert tickets. "Hmm . . ." I didn't have time to view them properly—because his speech was now moving at an accelerated pace and with a considerable rise in volume.

"Yes, Giry," he continued. "We're goin' to see POOL MAC 'ARTNEY EN WANGS at the Himmersmeeth Owdeeann 'morrow noit! Surprise!" He was now doing a bizarre roadside jig around me and my backpack, totally taken up in the spirit of giving—giving Wings tickets, that is. "I got theese off a tout! That show's been sold owt for wakes, but . . . You'll niver bay-leeve ate! WE'RE GOIN'!"

There they were—two matching little pieces of brightly colored cardboard with the magic words "Paul McCartney" and even that silly Wings logo inscribed on both. The solemn words beneath—"Odeon Hammersmith"—looked regal enough to impress even my faraway, doubting parents. The price? Expensive even by British standards. And who knows what service fee those dastardly scalpers slapped on top. Once it sank in, I struggled to find sufficient words of thanks.

"Gee," I said, spoken like a true Canadian. "I don't know what to say! These certainly are a surprise and are about the last thing I expected on my final day in England! These are . . . ," I looked again at the tickets, reading very carefully the fine print below the words "McCartney" and "Odeon." My spirit sank. "These are for . . . ," I said, looking again to make sure my eyes were seeing straight. "TOMORROW NIGHT!"

"Right! 'Morrow noit!" my young Aussie repeated, but he could sense something was amiss. "Sow?"

I tried not to sound too crestfallen as I said, "But I'm leaving *tomorrow morning.*"

This seemed the kind of pickle even Allan Williams couldn't babble his way out of. By the time the by-far-most-popular ex–Mop Top would be striking the first note of "Rock Show," I'd be on an Air Canada 747 turning left over Greenland. Oh, irony of ironies! My visitor's visa was about to expire and I had no money left to secure a later flight. I handed back the envelope to my friend, who now seemed far from jig-full. *You go, and have a real good time. . . . You stupid Dave Clark Five fan,* I thought. "Drop me a line and tell me how great the show was," I said, turning away.

I must have looked even more disheartened than I was trying to sound, because the Australian was having none of it. "Look 'ere mite . . . ," he said. (Those natives from down under really do say "mate" a lot.) "Yer flight's not 'til the wee hours of the mornin', right? En we're owl-redy close to Himmersmeeth, so let's jest gow bey the show toe-noit, 'ang 'round owtside en at leest try to 'ave some fun bey-fore you gow, right?" Yes, of course, he was right. London was a big town and I had almost the whole night ahead of me. There must be *some* trouble we could get into!

The fabled English sun had just set as we plowed headlong into the electric throng already

One of the many faces of Paul, who hams it up for "Jet." After the song he says, "Thank you very much and welcome to the Windy City. . . CHI-CA-GO!" June 1, 1976, Chicago Stadium, Chicago, Illinois.

◄ Paul, in deep concentration, plays a pulsating bass rhythm as he bounces to the beat. "Time to Hide," June 1, 1976, Chicago Stadium, Chicago, Illinois.

▲ "Venus and Mars," June 21, 1976, Forum, Inglewood, California. At this show Paul faked the introduction to "Yesterday." "See if you can remember this one. Oh, say can you see. . ." *[Sings the first few words from the "Star-Spangled Banner," drawing laughter from the audience]*

buzzing around the Odeon. In what must have been London's first major display of ex-Beatlemania, the adjoining streets and sidewalks were packed with excited, agitated fans. Many were dressed in oddly styled tartan scarves that can only be described as "glitter kilts"—impressively, a full eighteen months before Bay City Rollermaniacs took up similar garb. Our only hope was that this state of circus frenzy extended clear through the imposing doors of the concert hall itself, allowing us to enter the building without anyone of authority noticing tomorrow night's tickets in our hands.

Swept up in the crazed atmosphere of it all and knowing that the worst fate that could befall us was arrest and deportation, we strode defiantly up to the ticket taker who we thought had the worst set of eyes.

"Tickets please?" this weasely little man mumbled as we approached the doors.

"Uh, sure," we said, our brows dampening as our thumbs strategically covered the premature date on each stub. As a little luck would have it, he waved us on through without another word or a glance underthumb.

▲ A grimace from McCartney as he sings, "He's gonna wear you ow-out!" "Beware My Love," June 1, 1976, Chicago Stadium, Chicago, Illinois.

▶ "Tell you what. Do you fancy a bit of rock and roll?" Intro to "Hi Hi Hi," June 1, 1976, Chicago Stadium, Chicago, Illinois.

"Way deed ate! WAY DEED ATE!" my accomplice in concert-crashing yelled as we burst into the sumptuous splendor of the Odeon lobby. "DAMN! WAY GOT EN!"

We shoved toward the inner sanctum, where the enticing preshow chatter and last-minute microphone checking was becoming ever more audible. "You know, that was almost too easy," I couldn't help but add. And guess what? I was right.

I'm not sure if it was our telltale chorus of Australio-Canadian cackling that betrayed us, or our most conspicuous lack of tartan headgear, but when we heard an ominous shout of "'ERE, YOU TWO!" from behind, we knew it could only have been meant for us. We turned meekly, as a pair of security men pointed to the floor directly in front of them. "Step over 'ere NOW, you two," the meaner-looking one barked. Wearing our best hand-caught-in-the-cookie-jar faces, we obeyed. "Show us yer tickets," they commanded.

"Tickets? Oh yes, tickets," we said, grinning sheepishly. Unlike with the little old man we encountered outside, our thumbs were certainly no match whatsoever for the two men who now tore the cardboard slips nastily from us. Within ten seconds, after raising eyebrows toward one another, the big one said simply, "Right! OUT YOU GO!"

"I beg your pardon, kind sirs?" we squeaked. "These tickets aren't for this show!" one said, stating the pathetically obvious. "Yes, dear sir, they are," I lied. "It says right here, as I'm sure you can see, you FINE security person, 'Paul McCartney and Wings: Odeon Hammersmith.'"

"Yes, en thees is the Owdeeann Hammersmeeth?" my Australian added, to no real effect. "En that is Pool Mac 'Artney en Wangs pree-paring to perform en there . . . ."

"Yeah, it is," the big guy agreed as he placed a single arm firmly behind both our backs. "And out there is the gutter, where I'll be planting BOTH of your FINE ASSES if I 'ear another word from either of you little sh★ts!" The Odeon's security staff were most obviously trained in the deepest, darkest Brooklyn-speak, if the wording of this request was any indication.

"NOW SEE HERE!" I hollered (to great effect, as it turns out). "We've traveled HALF WAY AROUND THE WORLD to see this show! I've come from Canada, and my friend here has flown all the way from Australia. I'll be DAMNED if we're going to miss this show!"

"Then come back tomorrow night, why don't ya?" the smaller of the two security men answered, logically, of course, as they continued to propel us ever closer to the aforementioned street. "Use yer BLOODY tickets when yer supposed to."

"But way can't!" Australian Boy shouted, pointing toward my backpack. "Ee's gotta gow beck to Caneeda in the urly mornin'."

"Then ya better get a move on, or ee's gonna miss 'is plane," the goons larfed as they shoved us toward the door.

We thought we'd go out fighting, pushing, or clinging like spoiled little tourists to the oak doorframes of the Odeon, screeching, "No. No. We won't go. We wanna stay. We must see PAULIE!"

At the last possible second—before we became unglued from the edge of the building— another voice, and another arm, suddenly intervened. A far more refined voice this time and quite a finely tailored arm as well, we couldn't help but notice. "I'll take care of this now," this new character said. "Return to your post, gentlemen. And if you two young gentlemen wouldn't mind accompanying me . . . ."

After the goons were begrudgingly dismissed, we turned to find a tall, fairly immaculately dressed man with an oddly tanned (for Britain, that is) face beckoning us forward. Forward, that is, *inside* the building! This was definitely the direction for us. We followed him, not knowing our fate—but when had that ever stopped us before? He led us into a small office opposite the main entrance to the theater proper, where we were politely asked to wait as a door closed us in.

After five minutes, which seemed like five hundred, the door again opened. And who should return but the nice man with the odd tan who had interceded on our behalf already once. "The show is about to begin, so this can't take long," he said. "But can I see your tickets please?"

We duly produced the same, though by now they were more than a little worse for the wear from all our subterfuge and subsequent struggling. "Very good. And which of you is leaving the country?" he asked. I nodded nervously. "Then, if you are leaving early tomorrow, I trust you have your plane ticket with you now as well?" Indeed, I had. "May I see it please?" He could. "I

McCartney plays supporting bass for "Medicine Jar," sung by Jimmy McCulloch. Joe English pounds away on drums in the background. June 1, 1976, Chicago Stadium, Chicago, Illinois.

see. Well, all seems to be in order. Unfortunately, as you're no doubt well aware, tonight's performance is completely sold-out and these tickets cannot reserve you any seating, but if you will bear with me, I think I can help you out to some extent. Could you follow me again please? And do hurry, we haven't very much time at all."

He whisked us back out into the lobby, which was now emptying fast as the preconcert music began drifting out of the hall. "Umm, excuse me? Where are you taking us?" I asked. "Oh, my apologies!" he said with sincerity. "I should have explained. My name is Brian Brolly. I am Mr. McCartney's manager and I couldn't help but overhear that little ruckus you created at the door! You see, I had to check first, but if you wouldn't mind standing for the next two hours, I should be able to find a place for you both in the press section. But we must move quickly, so do come along!"

We were escorted into the pitch darkness, as the nicest manager I've ever known guided us deep into the Odeon. And with nothing more than a few well-placed renditions of "It's quite alright. . . . They're with me," we found ourselves amidst a crush of photographers and writers, mere feet from the stage, as the first notes of "Venus and Mars" filled the hall. "I hope you enjoy the show," Mr. Brolly said with a wink as he disappeared back into the darkness. You know, I never had the chance to say it then, but on behalf of both my long-lost Australian and myself: "Thanks!"

Before we regained our bearings, smoke and light rose overhead, followed by a tremendous roar from both onstage and off as Joe English, Jimmy McCulloch, Denny Laine, the former Linda Eastman, and that left-handed guy from the Beatles, exploded into the "Venus and Mars/Rock Show" medley. Sure, you can cynically dismiss such cliché theatrics as smoke bombs, lasers, and maybe even lyrics like "In my green metal suit I'm preparing to shoot up the city." Ah, but to be in the actual center of it all—in the press section, smack-dab in front of the stage—where it's next to impossible to resist the fervor, excitement, and NOISE of a good old-fashioned rock-and-roll show.

And in 1975 Wings were a damn good rock band. Flushed with the excitement of its first full-scale British tour and champing at the bit to sail the entire production over the pond to America, McCartney's band was nothing short of spectacular. Even the tritest portions of his repertoire hit hard with the kind of punch so often lacking on the recorded versions. Sure, barnstormers like "Jet," "Live and Let Die," and "Band on the Run" couldn't help but head straight for the gut, but even a coupling as ill-advised as "You Gave Me the Answer" and "Magneto and Titanium Man" now benefited immensely from the magnificent drumming and lead guitar work of Messrs. English and McCulloch. McCartney performed his songs close to perfection and finished practically each and every number with a joyous and heartfelt whoop for joy!

And did you know this was the first tour in which the band included a healthy dose of gems from the Lennon/McCartney songbook? Forever PR-conscious, Paul bowed to public pressure and performed not one, but an entire midshow set of Fab classics with each and every word executed Beatles-perfect. I must admit I wasn't the only one who stood in a state of near-suspended animation as Paul McCartney, atop a stool and accompanied only by his own guitar, performed "Yesterday" for the first time in a decade.

I was the only one, however, who couldn't resist shouting out a highly inappropriate cry of "John Lennon!" as the final faint notes of "Blackbird" hung in the air. Those in the press section laughed. The Cute Beatle stuck his tongue out at me.

Unfortunately, the concert soon came to an end and I had just enough time to bid a hasty "au revoir, matey" to my antipodean pal before grabbing a cab to the airport. Yet a couple of hours later, with "Soily" still ringing in my ears as the British Isles disappeared far below, I couldn't help but wonder how four Liverpool lads so deeply and indelibly affected so many of our lives.

And as I write these words this evening—now supposedly all grown up and living in New York City, but still lugging my worn copies of *Meet the Beatles* and *Revolver* around the world— one still-elusive question continues to haunt and confound me every time I hear a Beatles song, see a Beatles picture, or think a Beatles thought:

Gee, I wonder what ever happened to that Australian guy?

—GARY PIG GOLD

▶ A close-up of Paul, with his "doe-eyed" expression, singing "Let Me Roll It." One of three sold-out shows at the Chicago Stadium. June 1, 1976, Chicago, Illinois.

▼ "All right! Aaal RIGHT! I'd like to introduce to you these fellas you might have seen who have been helping us on horns all evening. I'd like to introduce 'em to you anyway. Starting over on the left there, we have a young gentleman who is from Louisiana, New Orleans, Sir Thaddeus Richard! Give a real big cheer, he likes it! And then coming this way a bit we have a gentleman here who's from Liverpool, England. His name is Howie Casey. And then coming over slightly this way we have a fellow who's from . . . you wouldn't exactly call him a gentleman, but he's a good lad. This fellow is from Dallas, Texas. That's Steve Howard. And then we have on the end, the midget of the group, from Macon, Georgia, on trombone, Tony Dorsey. They're gonna help us do a tune called 'Letting Go' man . . . ," June 1, 1976, Chicago Stadium, Chicago, Illinois.

My husband and I had just had our baby and we were desperately scraping money together. With the little money we had I only allowed myself to purchase Paul McCartney or Beatles records. My husband used to tell people about how true-blue I was to Paul and the Beatles. When I found out that Paul was coming to New York, it was so important for me to see him—it would make my life complete.

Getting tickets was tough and I ended up paying more than one week's salary for them. The tickets were $9.50 (face value), but the wormy ticket agent in Hackensack, New Jersey, wanted—and got—$33 apiece!

I had the most unbelievable time at the concert. A special moment happened right after the show. I took my little sister down to the stage perimeter. There were die hard fans waiting by the stage, savoring the McCartney concert experience.

One roadie picked up on our excitement and grabbed a guitar string on the floor near Paul's chair. "Here, CATCH!" he said, throwing Paul's guitar string toward us. The next few seconds were frozen in time. I felt the presence of a huge guy next to me, vying for the catch of the night. Both of us caught the guitar string at the same time. Instinct took over. I looked him straight in the eye as I furiously wound the metal guitar string around my hand. Taking full advantage of his ever-so-slight hesitation, I declared, "If you want this guitar string, you're going to have to take me with it!" The Big Guy didn't take long to relent. He knew he was dealing with a lunatic.

Seeing Paul in person is something words can't express. I still treasure the guitar string, along with my concert T-shirt and ticket stubs. I went home floating on air, remembering the thirty-plus songs he sang, logging every detail into the Beatles diary I still have today.

—LORENZA VIDRIS-NORTON

▶ "Thank you Los Angelians and various flowers. *['Flowers' was a nod to me, as I was waving a large bouquet in front of the stage.]* Listen, if anyone feels like tapping their toes, this is a toe-tapper. That's it! Got a hoedown here. This is going back a few years, so any over twelves in the audience should remember. . . ." Paul's introduction to "I've Just Seen a Face." June 21, 1976, Forum, Inglewood, California.

I SAW HIM

May 29, 1976, Kemper Arena, Kansas City, Missouri

A month before the show, some friends and I drove a distance of 175 miles to secure tickets that required many long hours waiting in line with hundreds of other McCartney fans. Tickets ranged from $7.50 to $9.50 and when they were finally in hand, we counted down the days to the concert.

On the day of the show, I arrived and saw scalpers asking $100 for third-row seats. I refused such offers—something I wouldn't think of these days.

Around 5:00 P.M. police motorcycles with sirens blaring approached the arena. A group of limousines drove into the parking lot as crowds began lining up. Paul's limo rolled by and he gave us the thumbs-up sign. The limo carrying Denny Laine stopped and out he came, waving to the crowd.

▲ Paul unleashes some fury with gutsy vocals on "Beware My Love." June 1, 1976, Chicago Stadium, Chicago, Illinois.

▶ Enveloped in fog, Paul appears in a heavenly beam of light as tiny bubbles fall from the ceiling. The dramatic "Venus and Mars/Rock Show" opener, June 21, 1976, Forum, Inglewood, California.

At 6:00 P.M. we could hear the band doing its sound check. "Lady Madonna" was played twice as we stood outside and thought, *Man, he's just inside this building!*

People arrived on foot or by vehicles decorated with McCartney photos taped to doors and windows. Solo McCartney and Beatles music filled the air as people gathered. The concert hadn't started yet and I was having the time of my life. I felt a closeness with this group of strangers who shared my love of McCartney and his music. These people could understand what I felt, share my thoughts, know that this was going to be a night to remember. After waiting twelve years, I was about to see my idol—the one and only PAUL McCARTNEY!

▲ A somber Paul sings one of five Beatles numbers, "Blackbird." The audience couldn't resist making birdcalls during the song, which brought a smile to McCartney's face. June 21, 1976, Forum, Inglewood, California.

▲ Paul and Linda croon on "Bluebird." "Does anyone know what a rhythm box is?" Paul asks. *[A few hands go up]* "It's this little box that you can get. You plug it into your wall and press a button. Can you hear it now? Turn it up lads! *[Sound of a repeating percussion is heard]* That's it, lovely stuff. Here you go! That's a rhythm box." June 21, 1976, Forum, Inglewood, California.

Eighteen thousand people jammed into the sold-out arena to witness what a writer for the *Kansas City Star* labeled "one of the best concerts ever seen in this town." When the lights went down, a thunderous roar erupted from the crowd. The musical journey had begun. I'll never forget the awesome sight of the blackened auditorium illuminated by thousands of camera flashes—so many that you could plainly see Paul and his band as they walked onstage. That moment is frozen in my memory and after twenty years I still get goose bumps each time I hear the opening notes to "Venus and Mars."

Fog began filling the stage floor as bubbles floated around the band. Images from the *Venus and Mars* album were projected on the ceiling and walls. Each band member fell into his or her own colored spotlight as Paul stepped up to the microphone and began to sing. A lone spotlight shone on him and I thought, *God, there he is!* Years of collecting McCartney memorabilia were now justified—with the reason standing right in front of me. Paul's voice and showmanship were perfection. Live renditions of the songs improved upon the album versions as the tight Wings lineup rocked the arena.

As the end of the show neared, I waited until "Band on the Run" to make the long haul to the backstage area—where I could watch the band walk to the dressing rooms. Surprisingly, no one else had the same idea. My friend and I leaned on the railing and watched below as each member of the band walked by. When Paul passed I reached over and patted him on the head— my way of telling him "Well done, Paul." With all the noise and commotion, I question whether Paul felt my compliment because he never reacted to my friendly pat.

I have seen some excellent concerts in my time, but without a doubt this was the most professional and magical show I have ever seen. The 1989–90 and 1993 shows were very special, indeed, but the 1976 Wings over America shows were the best for me. The success of this tour gave me the satisfaction of knowing that others had discovered what I knew all along— that McCartney's awesome talent and creative genius will not be surpassed in our lifetime.

—MICHAEL CUBA

June 4, 1976, Civic Center, St. Paul, Minnesota

▲ The back side of the pick used by Paul during the Wings concerts in 1976.

▶ Paul—surrounded by fan-patterned, green lasers—is dramatically bathed by an overhead spotlight during "Soily," the last number of the show. June 21, 1976, Forum, Inglewood, California.

▼ The McCartneys together at their keyboards sing "Magneto and Titanium Man," a lively song about comic-strip characters. June 1, 1976, Chicago Stadium, Chicago, Illinois.

I met Linda McCartney right after the Minnesota concert when I decided to have a closer look at the stage. Most of the audience had left and roadies were busy breaking things down. Paul's guitars were still there and I was admiring them when Linda unexpectedly walked onstage.

She was wearing sandals, a long denim skirt, a multi-colored knitted vest, and was holding a Polaroid camera. A member of the stage crew accompanied her and was having his picture taken. I called out, "Linda!" And she came right over to me and said, nonchalantly, "Yeah?" I asked if I could get a souvenir as a keepsake from the concert. She said, teasingly, "What would you like? One of Paul's guitars?" I told her that I'd like one of his guitar picks. She said, with a slight British accent, "You mean a plectrum?" I nodded. "Paul usually throws them on the ground near his microphone stand. Where was he standing tonight?" she asked. I pointed and said, "Right there!" Linda went over to the microphone and found four picks. She gave one to me and the rest to others who had gathered there. It was tortoiseshell red and said "Wings" on the front and "Manny's" (a guitar shop in New York City) on the back.

Noticing my *Wings over America* program, Linda kindly offered to autograph it. She bent down, asked my name, turned to the page that showed a photo of her with a koala bear, and signed it. I thought she looked very natural and had little or no makeup on.

Next she raised her Polaroid camera, snapped a picture of us, signed the back, and gave it to me. She said, "Is there anything else?" Someone asked where Paul was and Linda explained that he was doing a backstage interview with a Canadian radio station and they would be leaving right after that. Satisfied that she had fulfilled all our requests, Linda took more Polaroids of the stage. After finishing, she said goodbye and left.

I couldn't help but wonder, *Would she* really *have given me Paul's Rickenbacker?*

—DR. LAWRENCE DAVIS

▲ Paul purses his lips to the microphone, singing the "oohs" to "Jet." June 1, 1976, Chicago Stadium, Chicago, Illinois.

▶ McCartney pauses at the piano to let Linda introduce the next song. "I'll turn you over now to my wife and missus, Linda. Here she is." *[Applause]* Linda says, "Thank you. ALL RIGHT! This next song is about a secret agent who's from Great Britain. His name is James Bond, 007. It's called 'Live and Let Die.'" June 1, 1976, Chicago Stadium, Chicago, Illinois.

I SAW HIM

May 22, 1976, Boston Garden, Boston, Massachusetts

When the big day came, I raced to my seat just as the house lights went out and the opening chords to "Rock Show" began. Paul appeared in clear view as a spotlight illuminated him and the house went nuts.

During the show, a male fan jumped onstage, grabbing Paul in a bear hug. He took Paul's microphone and shouted to the crowd, "I can't help it. . . . I love Paul McCartney!" Security escorted this deliriously happy guy offstage. Paul found this very humorous and yelled, "I love him, too!"

I walked back to my car, thinking how great the evening had been. When I got there four black limos were lined up directly in front of my car. I sat there for a half hour just in case Paul might appear. Finally, they all took off together and I followed in my car. The parking lot was just about empty, so I parked the car and walked to a backstage door where two girls were waiting. I hoped a close encounter was imminent.

Drummer Joe English came out first, shook hands, signed autographs, and got into a limo. Next came guitarist Jimmy McCulloch, who said a few words before entering the same car.

Denny Laine came out and answered the question of the evening, saying, "Paul will be right out." My heart was pounding. Suddenly, from out of the darkness, a rowdy group of about forty people came running to the door. My heart began to sink when I realized that there was no way Paul and Linda could make it to their car through the crowd.

At that very moment, I heard someone yell "There he is!" only to see Paul and Linda exit from another door about thirty yards away and jump into the limo. They waved to us as they sped off.

I ran to my car and followed in pursuit, hoping to catch them at a hotel or the airport. I must have run three stoplights. But then someone cut in front of me and ended my adventure by stopping at the next light. I couldn't do anything except hold back the tears.

—JEFF LANDROCHE

November 13, 1975,
Myer Music Bowl,
Melbourne, Australia

Paul and Wings were playing a couple of nights in Melbourne on his Wings over Australia Tour. Since I could not afford a reserved seat, I camped out at the Music Bowl the night before the show.

During the night I chatted with the security guards who were patrolling the area. One of them gave me a hot tip: Paul would be arriving at Gate 7 at 2:00 P.M. for a sound check. WOW! I was sure I was the only person alive who knew this secret!

The next day, shortly before two, I slipped away from the crowd and made my way to Gate 7. Unfortunately, the security guard must have told every person he met. It was impossible to get near Gate 7, due to the large mob of people. The only spot left was about fifteen yards away from where I was sure Paul's limo would stop.

At 2:10, a sleek black limo carrying Paul and Linda stopped directly in front of me! I couldn't believe it! I was stunned. Fortunately, my reflexes took over and I jumped the rope fence, thrust my cassette recorder at Paul, and begged him to say something. Paul was a little surprised and said, with a smile, "Hello! How ya doin'? Alright?" As he was hustled off by security, he had a somewhat bemused look on his face.

Then Linda got out of the car and I yelled, "Linda! Linda! LINDA!" aiming the recorder in her direction. She responded with, "Hello! Hello! HELLO!" I could have kissed her, but at that moment I was pounced on by a burly security guard who threw me back over the barrier.

To this day I still cherish that cassette tape. The memory of those few moments remains as one of the best times of my life.

—ROSS HOBBS

▲ Paul grins at screaming fans who encourage him to do the "Macca March," an exaggerated strut performed by Paul during his hit song "Silly Love Songs." June 1, 1976, Chicago Stadium, Chicago, Illinois.

▶ A wide-angle shot of the band onstage performing the title song from McCartney's most successful Wings album, *Band on the Run*. "Listen, we're getting near the end of our show here this evening. Yes! YES! Thanks very much for coming. ESPECIALLY the people who came." June 1, 1976, Chicago Stadium, Chicago, Illinois.

I SAW HIM

May 7, 1976, Olympia Stadium, Detroit, Michigan

As a teenager, I worked for five years as a volunteer at Olympia Stadium for the Red Wings hockey games. My friends and I grew to know the staff quite well and had free entrance privileges. The bright idea to try and get into rock concerts dawned on us slowly. On the afternoon of the show the doormen just let us in, thinking we were going to work that night. No one questioned us so we headed toward the sound of a piano being tuned.

As we got closer I realized that the people onstage were not roadies! It was Paul, Linda, and the other members of Wings. By the time we got to the stage, Paul had left the piano and was strapping on a guitar. He wore a blue Hawaiian-print shirt and jeans. I couldn't tell you what Linda and the others were wearing, as I never took my eyes off Paul!

If all this wasn't enough, Paul spoke to us! He asked us to sit down so they could play us a tune to check the equipment. I looked around with a "who, me?" expression and he gestured to the seats. I realized he meant *us!*

As they started to play "Letting Go," I remembered I had brought my trusty Kodak Instamatic camera. I pulled it out and held it up hesitantly. I didn't want to offend Paul by taking his photo without asking, but this was my lucky day. His answer was to *wave* at me. So I snapped away while he mugged for the camera.

They finished playing and we clapped. He said, "See ya at the show." And then headed offstage. While it was happening, time seemed to stand still and then it was all over in a rush.

▲ "I feel like letting go," sings Paul. The McCartneys used Chicago as a home base during the Midwest segment of the tour, horseback riding every day on a farm in Mundelein that was provided by Arthur Wirtz (who owned the Chicago Stadium). "Letting Go," June 1, 1976, Chicago Stadium, Chicago, Illinois.

▶ Paul, seated at the piano, belts out his love song to Linda, "Maybe I'm Amazed." "Help me sing MAAAH song!" June 1, 1976, Chicago Stadium, Chicago, Illinois.

I could just kick myself now for not saying something, *anything!* I was in a fog. After Paul left, we rushed back to tell the switchboard girl about it and giggled and pinched ourselves until concert time.

Unfortunately my photographs turned out to be as wobbly as my knees. I know who is in the photos and I can remember how he looked when he sang to me. No one can take those few special moments away from me.

Even though it's been more than twenty-three years since that night, I still get a thrill just thinking of it. I can close my eyes, picture the stage and his smiling face, and get the feeling that he is standing there, playing and singing just for me. He has a way of making you feel you're the only person in the room.

This memory has the ability to pick me up when I'm down. I get a delicious shiver throughout my body when I recall it. I often find myself wondering if Paul realizes just how important all those small encounters are to his fans. I suppose he does, since he always takes time to interact with his fans. The pleasure he gives can never be measured with words. Thank you, Paul, for all that you do.

—Pat Sudds

42

Candids 1978–1984

▲ Paul arranges his own photo
session with me and a friend outside
Abbey Road Studios. "Ready?" he
asks. "One, two, three, CLICK!"

▶ McCartney signs an autograph for
my friend outside RAK Studios in
St. John's Wood, London, England.
October 6, 1978, *Back to the Egg*

◄ Paul points in my direction and tells me not to read a book that a fan has just asked him to autograph. He says, "Don't read this book. It's a terrible book!" McCartney and entourage were walking through the hotel lobby to the press conference where his new movie *Give My Regards to Broadstreet* was being launched. October 18, 1984, Chicago, Illinois.

► In the hotel lobby Paul signs autographs. Later he managed to surprise my friends and me when we were having a private conversation about him. He singled out one friend who had met him earlier and said, shaking a finger at all of us, "Don't believe a word she says!" October 18, 1984, *Give My Regards to Broadstreet* movie promotional tour, Chicago, Illinois.

1979-1988 CONCERT DATES

1979 UK November 23, 24, 25, 26: Royal Court Theatre, Liverpool, England • November 28, 29: Apollo in Ardwick, Manchester, England • December 1: Gaumont, Southampton, England • December 2: New Conference Centre, Brighton, England • December 3: Odeon, Lewisham, England • December 5: Rainbow Theatre, Finsbury Park, England • December 7, 8, 9, 10: Wembley Arena, Wembley Park, England • December 12: Odeon, Birmingham, England • December 14: City Hall, Newcastle-upon-Tyne, England • December 15: Odeon, Edinburgh, Scotland • December 16, 17: Apollo Theatre, Glasgow, Scotland • December 29: Concert for Kampuchea, Odeon Hammersmith, Hammersmith, England **1985 UK** July 13: Live Aid Concert, Wembley Stadium, Wembley Park, England **1986 UK** June 20: Prince's Trust Concert, Wembley Arena, Wembley Park, England **1988 ITALY** February 27: San Remo Song Festival, Teatro Ariston, San Remo, Italy

A blush-faced Paul, embarrassed by hotel employees applauding his entrance, gives them a salute. McCartney was in Chicago promoting his film *Give My Regards to Broadstreet.* Both he and Linda appeared on a television show called *AM Chicago,* which was hosted by a then virtually unknown Oprah Winfrey. October 17, 1984, Ambassador East Hotel, Chicago, Illinois.

1989-1990 CONCERT DATES

1989 REHEARSALS July 26, 27: London Playhouse Theatre, London, England • August 24: The Lyceum Theatre, New York, New York • September 21: Goldcrest Elstree Studios, Hertfordshire, England **1989 EUROPE** September 26: Drammenshallen, Drammen, Norway • September 28: Scandinavium Hall, Göteborg, Sweden • September 29, 30: Isstadion, Stockholm, Sweden • October 3, 4: Sporthalle, Hamburg, Germany • October 6, 7: Festhalle, Frankfurt, Germany • October 9, 10, 11: Palais Omnisports de Bercy, Paris, France • October 16, 17: Westfalenhalle, Dortmund, Germany • October 20, 21, 22: Olympiahalle, Munich, Germany • October 24: Palaeur, Rome, Italy • October 26, 27: Palatrussardi, Milan, Italy • October 29, 30: Hallenstadion, Zurich, Switzerland • November 2, 3: Palacio de los Deportes, Madrid, Spain • November 5: La Halle Tony Garnier, Lyon, France • November 7, 8, 10, 11: Ahoy Sportpaleis, Rotterdam, The Netherlands **1989 USA/CANADA** November 23, 24, 27, 28, 29: Forum, Inglewood, California • December 3, 4, 5 (filming of **48 Hours**): Rosemont Horizon, Rosemont, Illinois • December 7: Skydome, Toronto, Ontario, Canada • December 9: Forum, Montreal, Quebec, Canada • December 11, 12, 14, 15: Madison Square Garden, New York, New York

1990 UK January 2, 3, 5, 6, 8, 9: National Exhibition Centre (NEC), Birmingham, England • January 11, 13, 14, 16, 17, 19, 20, 21, 23, 24, 26: Wembley Arena, Wembley Park, England **1990 USA** February 1, 2: Palace of Auburn Hills, Detroit, Michigan • February 4, 5: Civic Arena, Pittsburgh, Pennsylvania • February 8, 9: Worcester-Centrum, Worcester, Massachusetts • February 12: Riverfront Coliseum, Cincinnati, Ohio • February 14, 15: Market Square Arena, Indianapolis, Indiana • February 18, 19: The Omni, Atlanta, Georgia **1990 JAPAN** March 3, 5, 7, 9, 11, 13: Tokyo Dome, Tokyo, Japan **1990 USA** March 29: Kingdome, Seattle, Washington • March 31 and April 1: Memorial Stadium, Berkeley, California • April 4: Sun Devil Stadium, Tempe, Arizona • April 7: Texas Stadium, Irving, Texas • April 9: Rupp Arena, Lexington, Kentucky • April 12: Tampa Stadium, Tampa, Florida • April 14, 15: Joe Robbie Stadium, Miami, Florida **1990 SOUTH AMERICA** April 20, 21: Maracana Stadium, Rio de Janeiro, Brazil **1990 UK** June 23: Scottish Exhibition Hall, Glasgow, Scotland • June 28: King's Dock Arena, Liverpool, England • June 30: Knebworth Festival, Knebworth Park, England **1990 USA** July 4, 6: R.F.K. Stadium, Washington, D.C. • July 9, 11: Giants Stadium, East Rutherford, New Jersey • July 14, 15: Veterans Stadium, Philadelphia, Pennsylvania • July 18: Cyclone Stadium, Ames, Iowa • July 20: Municipal Stadium, Cleveland, Ohio • July 22: Carter-Finley Stadium, Raleigh, North Carolina • July 24, 25 (filming of Get Back), 26: Sullivan Stadium, Foxboro, Massachusetts • July 29: Soldier Field, Chicago, Illinois

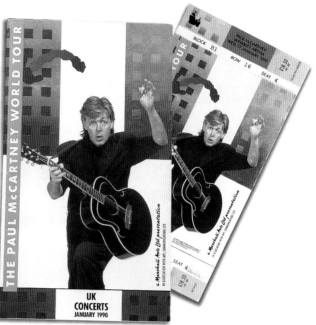

1989–1990 The Paul McCartney World Tour

IT HAD BEEN THIRTEEN YEARS since McCartney's last U.S. tour. With a new band and smash album *Flowers in the Dirt* (1989), Paul was back on the road again, playing sold-out shows. On this tour McCartney's band had no name. The official tour name was The Paul McCartney World Tour, a name so generic that the press dubbed it the Flowers in the Dirt World Tour, after his hit album.

The band lineup included: Robbie McIntosh (lead guitar, backing vocals), formerly of the Pretenders; Hamish Stuart (rhythm guitar, bass, backing vocals), from the Average White Band; Chris Whitten, a session drummer who worked on Paul's Russian album, *Choba B CCCP* (1991); Paul "Wix" Wickens (keyboards, backing vocals), who also worked with the Pretenders; and Paul's wife, Linda, (keyboards, percussion, and backing vocals). This was the best group of musicians McCartney had performed with since his 1976 Wings over America Tour.

Tickets were priced at $28.50 for the duration of the tour, with the final show at Chicago's Soldier Field costing $32.50. Vendors sold T-shirts, jackets, sweatshirts, hats, pins, buttons, CDs, books, and programs. Everyone who attended received a lavish ninety-eight-page free program containing numerous photos with detailed biographical information about McCartney, his band, and crew.

The set consisted of twenty-nine songs plus one instrumental, and included fifteen Beatles tunes—a departure from the 1976 tour, where only five Beatles songs were performed. Paul had come to grips with his Beatles past—much to the delight of his audiences, who showed their appreciation by screaming at the first note of a Beatles song. Six songs were featured from the new *Flowers in the Dirt* album: "Figure of Eight," "Rough Ride," "We Got Married," "Put It There," "This One," and "My Brave Face."

McCartney's set list remained much the same throughout the ten-month world tour, with some songs dropped in favor of others. The first leg of the U.S. and U.K. tour included: "Figure of Eight," "Jet," "Rough Ride," "Got to Get You into My Life," "Band on the Run," "Ebony and Ivory," "We Got Married," "Maybe I'm Amazed," "The Long and Winding Road," "The Fool on the Hill," "Sgt. Pepper's Lonely Hearts Club Band," "Good Day Sunshine," "Can't Buy Me Love," "Put It There," "Things We Said Today," "Robbie's Bit" (instrumental), "Eleanor Rigby," "This One," "My Brave Face," "Back in the U.S.S.R.," "I Saw Her Standing There," "Twenty Flight Rock," "Coming Up," "Let It Be," "Ain't That a Shame," "Live and Let Die," and "Hey Jude." These songs were followed by an encore of "Yesterday," "Get Back," and "Golden Slumbers/Carry That Weight/The End."

By the latter part of the tour "Maybe I'm Amazed" and "Ebony and Ivory" were omitted. "Let 'Em In" and "Birthday" were added and Paul's short-lived version of "P.S. Love Me Do" (a new medley of the Beatles's songs "Love Me Do" and "P.S. I Love You") was quickly dropped due to audience ambivalence. "Twenty Flight Rock," a fan favorite, was also dropped—except for McCartney's final show in Chicago, on July 29, where he deemed it "appropriate" (because of the lyric "sent to Chicago"). "Mull of Kintyre" was performed only in Glasgow, Scotland.

These changes stemmed from Paul's overbooked tour schedule, which kept his vocals in a constant state of flux. The heavy demands of a two-and-one-half-hour show put a tremendous strain on his voice. Many of the shows were back-to-back, not giving Paul's vocal cords a chance to rest. McCartney, however, overcame these limitations after a brief rest before the start of the stadium shows on the last leg of his American tour (July 1990).

McCartney's concerts all began with an eleven-minute movie short by famed director Richard Lester (*A Hard Day's Night, Help!*), which introduced new fans to Paul's eventful career. Musical clips of the Beatles and of Paul's solo years contained concert footage, home movies, historic events (of the era), and photos alternating on three enormous projection screens. While the audience was treated to this nostalgic trip through time, green lasers bombarded the stadium walls, building anticipation for McCartney's arrival onstage. The end of the film featured graphic images of animals being tortured,

Wembley Arena in Wembley Park, near London, England, where Paul performed eleven sold-out shows in January 1990. The billboard was unique to this venue. Colored lights of gold and blue lit up the sign at night. Searchlights panned the evening sky and could be seen for miles.

"We Got Married," April 15, 1990, Joe Robbie Stadium, Miami, Florida. At the previous night's show, Paul asked, "How 'bout them Dolphins then, hey?" He was answered with "boos" from disgruntled fans of the Dolphins football team, which was not doing well that season. "It's always a mistake to mention the football team," he conceded, adding, "So we won't!" Then with an American accent, he imitated the audience and said, "Boooo! I hate them! I hate them!" He continued, candidly, "I was talking about the tunas!" (referring to the controversy about dolphins drowning in nets used to harvest tuna).

evoking gasps of horror from the crowd—a strong statement on behalf of the McCartneys, who during this decade became crusaders for animal rights. The last frame of the movie showed the band as it would appear seconds later, preceded by the giant letters N-O-W. As the audience's expectations increased, they were further fueled by clouds of fog—which were pumped onto the stage, adding a dreamlike atmosphere. Then McCartney casually walked across it, waving to his admirers.

Screams reminiscent of a Beatles concert rose into a crescendo of sound—muted only by the deep drone of keyboards—as the opening chord of "Figure of Eight" filled the stadium. A youthful-looking forty-seven-year-old McCartney, dressed stylishly in a black military jacket (similar to the Beatles jacket he wore at New York's Shea Stadium in 1965), donned his Wal five-string bass, stepped up to the microphone, and began to sing. This new song from the *Flowers in the Dirt* album was a spectacular opener and McCartney, an astute showman, created a special "Figure of Eight" dance—shuffling his feet while following an imaginary eight-pattern on the stage floor, much to the amusement of the audience.

"OH YEAH! If there's anybody who's got a little bit of energy left and you want to dance some more, I'll tell you what we'll do then. We have a song that features our drummer, young Master Christopher, who will thrash about in a meaningful way. This song is called 'Coming Up.'" April 15, 1990, Joe Robbie Stadium, Miami, Florida.

Musical highlights were "Coming Up" and "We Got Married," with the former introduced as a number "featuring our drummer, young Master Christopher, who will thrash about in a meaningful way." A rowdy McCartney continued with a rash of silly dancing that involved touching his heels as he hopped around in circles, mock boxing gestures, uncoordinated hand and leg movements, and the occasional locked-elbow dancing with Robbie. Linda was raised high above the stage by a hydraulic lift beneath her keyboard platform. From there she encouraged crowd participation with waves and peace signs.

Lighting expert Marc Brickman brought his artistry to the McCartney tour with computerized light banks that created special effects with lasers, fog, and grid projections. "We Got Married" used highly sophisticated green lasers with crisscross grids that surrounded the stage perimeter as patterned spotlights of circles moved across the floor and ceiling.

Paul and Hamish Stuart slide across the stage on their knees, playfully nudging Robbie McIntosh, who tries hard to ignore them while playing the guitar solo. "We Got Married," April 15, 1990, Joe Robbie Stadium, Miami, Florida.

Paul opened the song with a sustained operatic vocal that provoked giggles from female fans. At one point, a rambunctious McCartney and Stuart slid on their knees across the stage to McIntosh, who played an inspired guitar solo in spite of Paul's and Hamish's playful nudging.

"The Fool on the Hill," a song dedicated to "three mates of mine—John, George, and Ringo—without whom . . . ," showcased Paul on his psychedelic piano, which revolved high above the crowd. Quotes from Martin Luther King's "I Had a Dream" speech echoed in the background.

Brian Clarke, the artist who designed the cover for the *Flowers in the Dirt* album and *Tug of War* (1982), employed thirty-six-foot-high abstract backdrops of colorful interlocking grids—a recurring visual theme used throughout the tour. The concept was to show an infinite space that would transcend the boundaries of the giant screens to an alternate world ordered by repetition of form. Lighting and music would complete the perfect concert atmosphere.

"I'd like to dedicate this song to three mates of mine—John, George, and Ringo—without whom. . . ." Paul's introduction to "The Fool on the Hill." April 15, 1990, Joe Robbie Stadium, Miami, Florida.

The Japanese tour (March 1990), South American tour (April 1990), and the third leg of the U.S. tour (April 1990) featured a new number called "P.S. Love Me Do." This combination of the Beatles's "P.S. I Love You" and "Love Me Do" was given a different arrangement and a disco beat. Paul introduced the song by saying, "This is my chance to bop along with you and put down my guitar and piano." Indeed, this song was a departure for McCartney—with just a handheld wireless microphone, sans guitar, Paul serenaded the crowd, leaping, dancing, and waving his hands.

Paul's tribute to John Lennon, whom he referred to as "a dear friend," was a medley of the Beatles's songs "Strawberry Fields" and "Help!" combined with Lennon's "Give Peace a Chance." The undulating sea of penlights magically appeared as fans wept, while others held a loved one close during this emotional tribute to the slain Beatle.

At all of the shows Paul plugged his favorite environmental charity, Friends of the Earth, by encouraging people to tell their politicians that they want to "live in a clean world." At a London show one drunken spectator yelled something unintelligible during the speech. Paul found this very amusing and retorted, "Shut up! You're not part of the act!"

In Chicago, the last show on the tour, McCartney humorously introduced his band. "How ya doing? Okay? This is the last night of our tour, you know, so we don't care anymore. I'll tell you what . . . I'd like to introduce you to the people on this stage, without whom I couldn't have done this show. We'll start over here. On guitar we have a young man called Robert Mac-In-CRUSH! Back here on the keyboards, we have Mr. Paul Wickens. GO WIX! When we were doing rehearsals for this show at this point the crowd was supposed to be shouting, WIX! WIX! WIX! So DO IT! *[Crowd chants, 'WIX, WIX, WIX!']* Okay! That's ENOUGH! I told you it would happen! *[Looks at Wix]* On drums, thrashing about as ever, young Chris Whitten, YO! *[Crowd's applause builds]* Over on the other keyboard here we have this young lady I've known for quite awhile. *[Points to Linda]* Miss Gertrude Higgins! GO GERTRUDE! She says that's not her name, but I don't believe it! And over in this corner, weighing three pounds and two ounces, the welterweight champion of Chicago—Hamish Stuart!"

McCartney, a merciless tease, faked the intro to "Hey Jude." "So, I'll tell you what . . . There's a bit at the end of this next song that you might just want to join in with. Okay? It goes like this. . . ." Instead of singing the opening words to "Hey Jude," McCartney would play either Van McCoy's "The Hustle" or "If I Were Not upon the Stage," an old British music-hall number. It brought laughter and cries of encouragement from the crowd. He stopped himself after a few bars and commented, "No! No! NO! We don't DO that one!" waving his hands at the band to stop. "A little mistake there. I know what we meant. A very similar song in some respects." Then he laughed and played his most popular Beatles song.

For the last song McCartney chose the *Abbey Road* medley of "Golden Slumbers/Carry That Weight/The   End." Starting on keyboards, Paul played the familiar chords with Linda flashing   the peace sign at his side. As the well-known drum solo began,

Paul and "Gertrude Higgins" (Linda's pseudonym for the tour) taking their bows after "Hey Jude." July 29, 1990, Soldier Field, Chicago, Illinois.

McCartney left the keyboard, grabbed his Gibson Les Paul guitar, and began a dueling jam with Hamish and Robbie, alternating lead guitar licks. The pace quickened as the trio furiously traded guitar solos, with McCartney, who churned out an impressive, hard-driving lead guitar, pushing his power-riffing mates across the stage. On the final note, the rock star leaped into the air and bid his audience farewell.

By the end of the ten-month tour McCartney had traveled 100,331 miles through thirteen countries, played 102 concerts, with forty-six sold-out performances in four continents to 2,843,297 people. He sold the most stadium concert tickets in the United States for that year, averaging 49,209 per show, surpassing Madonna, Janet Jackson, and the Grateful Dead. His Rio de Janeiro, Brazil, show set a new world record for the largest attendance at a stadium concert—184,368—breaking Frank Sinatra's previous attendance record. *Performance* magazine voted his tour the "International Tour of the Year" while *Billboard* magazine's sister publication *Amusement Business* honored him with an award for the highest grossing shows of 1990—the two Berkeley (California) Memorial Stadium concerts—which brought in $3,550,660. McCartney's album from the tour, *Tripping the Live Fantastic* (released in November 1990), quickly went platinum in the United States with sales of more than one million. It was McCartney's most successful tour and would not be his last.

"See ya next time!" Paul's final words as he leaves the stage, clapping in unison with the crowd. That was the last time he performed in Chicago. July 29, 1990, Soldier Field, Chicago, Illinois.

August 24, 1989, The Lyceum Theatre, New York, New York

In August of 1989, before Paul's Flowers in the Dirt World Tour, he rehearsed in New York. A local radio station was running a contest so that listeners could win tickets to this event. Every hour, the one hundredth caller would get two passes to watch the rehearsal. It was a Thursday and I was at work with my workmates who had radios. Knowing my love for Paul, they tried calling in for me all day long. Then, at 3:50 P.M., one of my coworkers was the one hundredth caller! The free pass had to be claimed by 5:00 P.M. and I was an hour away from New York City. Where was I going to put my car?

Determined not to miss this opportunity, I drove 90 mph on U.S. Route 208 and the New Jersey Turnpike. The gods were with me—no speeding tickets and no traffic in the Lincoln Tunnel, although I did drive on the sidewalk on Seventh Avenue. When I got to the Lyceum Theatre, I saw police on horses, barricades, and thousands of people lined up to see Paul. Looking at my watch, I realized it was 4:55 P.M. . . . only FIVE minutes to claim my pass! I left my new car in the middle of the street, shouted to a guy who looked like the garage attendant to "Take my car! I'll be back eventually," and ran down the middle of the street to the radio van, just as they were about to pull away. With two passes in hand, I gave one to a guy with puppy-dog eyes and we went in.

There were a few hundred people in the theater and Paul was already onstage rehearsing. As we were escorted to the front, I had to keep pinching myself because I couldn't believe Paul was two feet in front of me! I started to cry and he made a "boo-hoo" funny face at me.

He rehearsed on and off for almost two hours. During breaks, he and Linda would talk to us. I kept touching his shoe and he shook his finger at me and said, "If I can't touch *your* shoe, you can't touch *mine!*" So, I took my shoe off and held it up for him to touch.

It was over all too soon. And, yes, my car was waiting for me in the garage. I gave the attendant a $25 tip and literally flew home.
—ALICE KLEIN

◄ Paul sings "I Saw Her Standing There" with a mock surprised look as the crowd goes wild. February 14, 1990, Market Square Arena, Indianapolis, Indiana.

► McCartney holds his acoustic guitar high overhead as he acknowledges the applause after "Yesterday"–the most-played song in the world, with seven million airplays and recorded by more than 2,500 performers. February 14, 1990, Market Square Arena, Indianapolis, Indiana.

The McCartneys pause on their way to the press area backstage at Chicago's Soldier Field, July 29, 1990. This was the last show on the 1989–90 tour and where I gave Paul my book of photographs. Ten days later his office called and asked to use one of the photos on his new album. The publicist said, "We urgently need the photo and are holding up production of the album for it."

I SAW HIM

March 5, 1990, Tokyo Dome, Tokyo, Japan

In November of 1989 VH1 ran a contest for tickets to see Paul's concert in Japan and meet him backstage. I sent in more than three hundred postcards and, on January 2, I received a call that I had WON! For months I tried to figure out what to ask him. I couldn't come up with anything that wasn't too personal—the problem with having read or seen every book and magazine since 1964 with his name attached to it.

On March 5, my friend Allison and I were driven to the Tokyo Dome in a limo sent by Paul's people. At the stadium we were met by Fiona Hurry, Media Coordinator for the tour, and taken into a guest room to await Paul.

While we waited, we listened to Chris Whitten (Paul's drummer) give a magazine interview. Then we were taken backstage. Inside a room we saw James and Stella (McCartney's children)

saying goodbye to mom and dad—hugs and kisses all around. Just as the kids were about to leave we heard a familiar voice say, "Wait! You've got to hear this!" A young Japanese boy was playing "I Saw Her Standing There" on a Hofner bass. Right in front of us was this silly man dancing and shaking his rear end. It was none other than Paul.

The boy and Paul's kids left as we entered. I wondered how I should address him. Should I say "Mr. McCartney" or "Paul"? But in the end when he said "Hi, Bonnie!" I didn't even think. "Hi, Paul!" seemed as natural as breathing. He stepped forward and shook my hand. Just as he seemed about to step back, he leaned forward again and kissed me on my cheek! I'm not even sure if I was breathing at this point—since I was more concerned about crying, falling, or knocking him over. It was my first favorite Macca moment.

I noticed Linda on a sofa along the back wall, doing an interview with a woman journalist. She spoke to us from time to time. Paul asked us where we were from and was amused that I was from California and Allison was from New Hampshire. He kept singing "party, party . . . coast to coast" at odd moments and signed a group photo for us, plus a program and some postcards I had brought for my kids. They were fan club postcards and he asked, "Oh, you're fans then?" We said, "Oh, YES!" Paul's manager, Richard Ogden, said, "Well, it's a good thing you won then." And we agreed.

Paul gave each of us a two-CD set of *Flowers in the Dirt*. I couldn't think of much to say and was happy just to be there—staring as hard as I could, memorizing every detail of that man. With him being four inches away it was heaven! Slowly I realized that someone was saying, "Look at the camera. Look at the camera . . . ," which explains the lovely expression I'm wearing in the photo I received a year later from VH1!

At some point while Allison was chatting about various concerts Paul turned to include me in the conversation by giving me the most wonderful wink. It was my second favorite Macca moment. Yes, I know it's his thing and all that, but when it's directed at you, what a wondrous thing it is! He was warm, soft, and wonderful. But, alas, I couldn't tell you what he smelled like.

—BONNIE MULLEN

Paul and Linda pose backstage at Chicago's Soldier Field prior to the press conference and show. The couple was an hour and a half late arriving in Chicago due to a thunderstorm and missed the sound check. After the show there was a backstage party with a country and western band and vegetarian cuisine. In attendance were VIPs, friends, relatives, crew, and guests. The party lasted until almost 4:00 A.M. July 29, 1990, Soldier Field, Chicago, Illinois.

My husband found a ticket broker with second-row seats for the upcoming July 20 show in Cleveland. The tickets cost $150 each. We had never done anything so extravagant before, but we decided to go for it. And it was worth it! The seats were incredibly close to the stage with an unobstructed view and that night I learned about the power of distraction.

I had to use the rest room before the concert started. Hordes of people were pushing their way down to the seats as I was climbing up the stairs in search of a rest room. After fifteen minutes I still hadn't made it up the stairs and heard the famous first chord that started the preconcert film. There was *no way* I was going to miss Paul's entrance! I turned around and fought my way back to my seat just in time to see the film end.

It drizzled on and off during the show, but never really rained. During "The Long and Winding Road" Paul's mike went out and he made a joke—saying, "talk amongst yourselves"—as the roadies sprang into action. For the encore, the band came out in Cleveland Indian uniforms.

I didn't get to the rest room until after the show. When Paul took the stage, I forgot all about it! I was in total awe of that man and what a thrill it was.

—DEBORAH HEYL

◄ Paul pantomimes with silly gestures after "Live and Let Die," then leans against the piano as the crowd roars with approval. July 29, 1990, Soldier Field, Chicago, Illinois.

▲ McCartney gathers flowers and gifts from fans at the end of his performance. One lucky fan is thrown a prized pick from the star. July 29, 1990, Soldier Field, Chicago, Illinois.

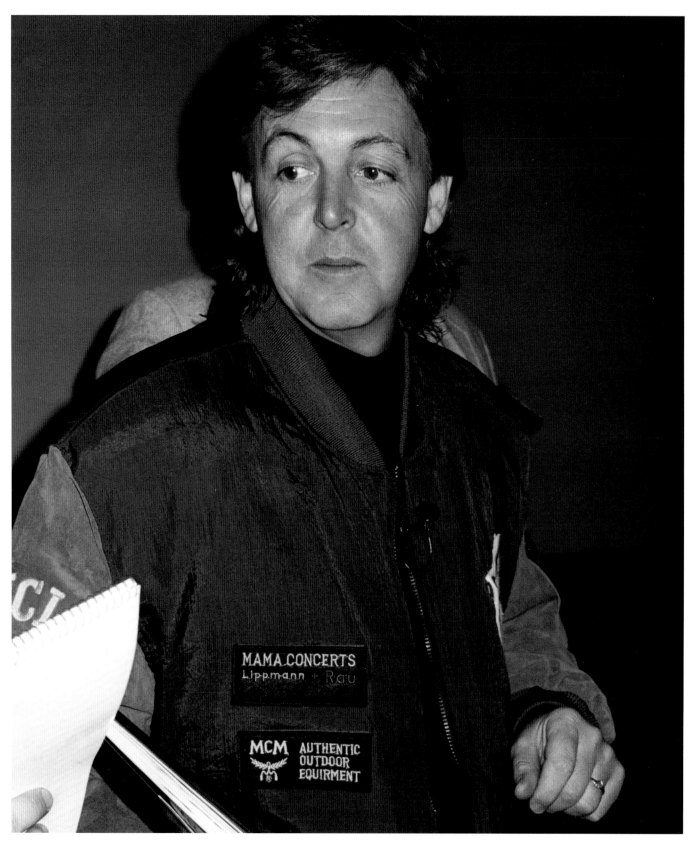

MAMA CONCERTS
Lippmann + Rau

MCM AUTHENTIC
OUTDOOR
EQUIRMENT

McCartney eyes a fan's notebook, offered for an autograph in the Skyline Room adjacent to the Rosemont Horizon, prior to the December 4, 1989, show. Paul was on his way to the press conference. Rosemont, Illinois.

I SAW HIM

December 3, 4, and 5, 1989, Rosemont Horizon, Rosemont, Illinois, filming of *48 Hours* and February 9, 1990, Worcester-Centrum, Worcester, Massachusetts

I received a phone call from a friend of mine who told me he was just interviewed by CBS for a *48 Hours* program featuring Paul McCartney. They needed a "real fan" who would follow Paul around Chicago when he did his three sold-out concerts at the Rosemont Horizon on December 3, 4, and 5. My friend gave them my phone number.

I was interviewed by various assistants and show producers via phone. They asked all types of questions about Paul and the Beatles. Then the head producer for *48 Hours* came over to my apartment and interviewed me, looked over the place, and asked more questions about my collection of Beatles records and memorabilia. I told him when he left to make sure they chose someone who really loved the Beatles and Paul. If they just picked anyone, we (the fans) would see right through the phony enthusiasm and it would destroy their story.

Later that week I got the call—they decided to have me be the *48 Hours* "fan." The camera crew came out to my apartment, wired me for sound, and set things up so that they could follow me around everywhere. It all went well, but I soon grew weary from the constant lack of privacy. They followed me to the hairdresser, the clothing store, Paul's hotel—where his limo pulled out of the underground parking area and I got a wave. Then I was videotaped driving to the Rosemont Horizon with a cameraman lying on the hood of my speeding car. He was taping me right through the windshield!

When the show was aired at the end of January in 1990, I couldn't believe how much my friends and I were on camera! After it was over, I received a phone call of thanks from the staff at CBS in New York and a souvenir *48 Hours* baseball cap. Later, I became sort of a celebrity in the Chicago area—with more than my fifteen minutes of fame. It's an interesting phenomenon, fame. One moment people want your autograph and the next moment you're home taking out the garbage.

I thought the program would make a nice video to show the next generation of relatives, but something unexpected happened. I received a phone call at my office from Paul's London publicist, Geoff Baker. He said that after Linda saw the program Paul decided that he wanted to meet me. Later I found out it was Linda's idea. If it weren't for her, I would never have met Paul. *Wow!* I thought, then I almost hung up, thinking it was a joke by one of my friends.

Paul and Linda pose arm in arm for the Chicago press. When asked if he had a chance to see the city without being bothered, Paul said, "See the city? I can do that. I'm always able to do that. In fact, the last time I was here, I was jogging along the bay [Lake Michigan] in the morning. It's just something I've always liked. I came from a very warm family upbringing in Liverpool, so I've never really been freaked by a crowd of people." December 4, 1989, Skyline Room of the Rosemont Horizon, Rosemont, Illinois.

It's funny how things happen in life. Back in February of 1964, I'm on the floor at home watching the Beatles's first appearance on the *Ed Sullivan Show* and on the very same day twenty-six years later (February 9, 1990) I'm on a plane with my husband, Bob, going to Worcester, Massachusetts, to meet Paul!

Paul and Linda paid for everything—the first-class plane trip, limo, hotel in Worcester, food, phone bills (sorry Paul), and tickets for the show. But the best part was the special VIP backstage passes to meet the McCartney brood! We met their son, James, and daughter Stella.

After the sound check, Paul came up to our seats and said, "I've heard all about you!" "I've heard a lot about you, too!" I replied. He was doing the typical rock star thing, strutting around, all zipped up in his "N-O-W" tour jacket and looking very handsome. His hazel eyes were absolutely gorgeous and I felt like I was staring at him. He was everything I expected him to be. Nice, fun, and sweet. "How are you doing, babe? All right? Nice to see you. You're the star of the show, I heard," he said. Then he gave me a kiss on the cheek and with very weak knees I gave him a few presents. He mumbled a few "dears" and "sweethearts" and talked about how he hadn't seen the *48 Hours* show yet.

Even though there were a few media people backstage, Paul made sure we had "private time" together. We spent about two hours with Paul, Linda, her sister Louise and brother, John, in the backstage dressing room. Nice people. Paul was great. He took so much time to talk, sign

▲ The highlight of this song was Paul strumming his guitar in close proximity to the fans. He hopped on platforms that extended from the stage into the photo pit. "Things We Said Today," December 4, 1989, Rosemont Horizon, Rosemont, Illinois.

◄ A pensive Paul in half-shadow puts his bass down after "Get Back" and gets ready to sing the last song of the evening. December 4, 1989, Rosemont Horizon, Rosemont, Illinois.

autographs, and make sure we were enjoying ourselves. At one point Paul asked me where my camera was. I said, "You guys have had enough of camera flashes and hounding!" Linda said, "How considerate!" Paul actually went out of their dressing room to fetch a photographer, who took lots of photos of us together. He also had the entire band sign an album for me.

Linda asked about our wedding anniversary. When I told her it was in March, she yelled over to Paul about how close our anniversaries were. Paul also gave me an armful of T-shirts, sweatshirts, postcards, and, of course, a few promotional records! The best was a *Flowers in the Dirt* promo poster that said, "Cheers to my costar, Joy. Love from Paul McCartney." I will always cherish that.

Our conversation covered life, family, and other things that were important. I scolded him at one point, saying "Where have you been? You're like family to me." After our meeting I was delighted to hear what Paul said to a local television station. He said, "I kind of feel like an elder brother . . . you know. . . . That's what Joy said. She felt like she's kind of known me for a long time. It's a funny little relationship you get . . . with nice fans."

This was, next to the day I got married, the happiest day of my life.

—Joy Waugh-O'Donnell

Paul sings the "oohs" to "Jet," backlit by yellow, blue, and red spots. He checks the audience's reaction as nervous sweat trickles down his cheeks. The crowd was dazzled by McCartney's spectacular performance in Chicago, December 5, 1989, Rosemont Horizon, Rosemont, Illinois.

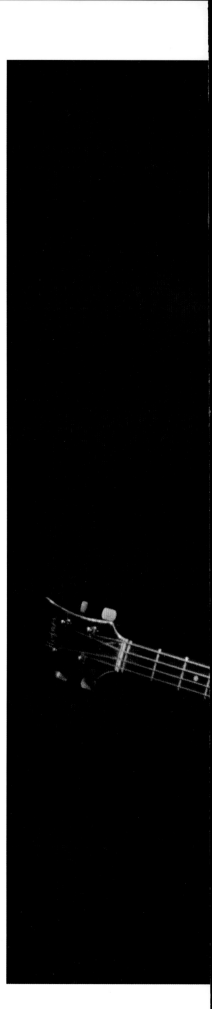

I SAW HIM

April 14, 1990, Joe Robbie Stadium, Miami, Florida

It was the show you couldn't get a ticket for, yet I had a front-row seat for Beatle Paul as he arrived to address members of the South Florida press on a humid Saturday afternoon. In just a few hours McCartney and his band would light up Miami's Joe Robbie Stadium with two and one-half hours of Beatles, Wings, and solo hits. I taped my microphone to Paul's and found a place to sit. Paul greeted the room with a friendly smile and a wave before taking his seat behind a long table.

He looked tanned and youthful in faded jeans, white golf shirt, and black jeans jacket. He gave the okay sign and began to field questions about his Friends of the Earth campaign, the deal with tour sponsor Visa, and his memories of South Florida. The last time Paul performed here he was a member of the most popular rock group in history. Back on that second historic Sunday in February of 1964, Paul and his mates played a ballroom at the Miami Deauville Hotel for the second *Ed Sullivan Show.* And twenty-six years later, he was back with a new band and a catalog of hits, some never performed live.

Most memorable was Paul's ability to volley back any question with a snappy answer and a smile. Nothing rattled him. Even a question about his favorite Lennon song brought a glance upward and a sensitive answer. (It's "Strawberry Fields" by the way, with "Beautiful Boy" taking a close second.) There was a moment of laughter when a reporter who questioned the high price of tickets ($28.50 at the time) was referred to Cher's ticket price, which exceeded the Cute Beatle's by a few dollars. Some highlights include:

Paul: Alright! Thank you, O-kaay! Good afternoon. How you doing? It's good here, isn't it? Hey? Good weather.

Q: I heard you were out at the Everglades yesterday. How did that go? Did you see any alligators?

Paul: That was nice. I saw one alligator, so my trip is complete and I reckon it was about twenty feet long, but they tell me it was more like six. I'm sticking 'round to about eighteen or so, I think, in the final analysis. It was very good, actually. We went out there to shoot a sequence for CBS's *Earth Day Special.* I just got a chance to kind of say "save the planet" as a scene in the Everglades kind of thing. Nice backdrop. *[Reporter formally introduces himself]*

Paul: *[Teases him for grandstanding]* This is HIM folks! In case you were in any doubt. THIS IS MIKE!

Mike: Having been a fan yourself, with so many fantastic artists when you were young, like Chuck Berry, Fats Domino, Little Richard . . . . Do you have any thoughts of having your own record label . . . or producing young artists . . . ?

Paul: Well, I'll tell you the thing about having your own record label: It's a lot of hard work. We did it with Apple Records and we had some nice records like *Hey Jude* and *Those Were the Days* and stuff, but in actual fact, it's a real time-consumer and at the moment I couldn't think of anything like that. I just haven't got the time.

Mike: What about the possibility of perhaps producing somebody?

Paul: Well, you know that's always a possibility, but I got to kind of be thrilled with their work to do it, 'cause generally I'm kind of too busy with what I'm doing myself these days. There was a time, 'round about Apple Records, when I did produce a lot of other people, but that was 'cause things were pretty light. We didn't have a lot on over the year, you know. It was kind of making an album and that was it. So, I had a lot of spare time. Now on tour, spare time is a thing of the past.

McCartney gestures to a fan to behave herself! "Twenty Flight Rock," July 29, 1990, Soldier Field, Chicago, Illinois.

Mike: How does an artist get the material?

Paul: *[Feigning annoyance]* IS THIS YOUR WHOLE SHOW, MIKE? Or . . . *[Addresses reporters]* Should Mike now sit down? *[Begins to chant]* Yeaah! SIT DOWN! SIT DOWN! GO MIKE! GO AWAY! *[Mike gets the message and sits down]* Thank you, Mike. You were great! Thanks, mate! Lovely!

Joe: **Joe Johnson from Majic 102.7. What are your memories of Miami twenty-six years ago?**

Paul: Oh, it was magic, because it was the first time we ever came out to anywhere this kind of tropical. What do I remember? I remember seeing our first American cop on his motorbike, you know, which we all immediately took photos of. We were so amazed! WOW! He was riding alongside us. We just had a great time. MG, the British motor car manufacturer, lent us an MG for the week—each. And we were just young kids you know, so that totally spaced us out, that one.

Joe: **Were you able to blend in with everybody and kind of go unnoticed?**

Paul: We went a little bit unnoticed, not totally unnoticed. I mean, we looked fairly different from the Miami crowd at that time. But we had a lot of fun. We really had a good few days here and a nice concert and stuff. . . .

Paul croons to "I Saw Her Standing There" at the 102nd and last show of the tour, July 29, 1990, Soldier Field, Chicago, Illinois.

Joe: Has it changed?

Paul: Well, in fact, I haven't been into Miami yet. It's all kind of moved out, isn't it? I haven't actually been down there, so I can't really tell you how much it's changed. But it's obviously growing like mad.

Q: I heard that Michael Jackson would turn the music [the Beatles's song catalog] back over to you if the Beatles reunited.

Paul: Who dreamed that one up?

Q: Michael Jackson, reportedly.

Paul: REPORTEDLY? *[Looks at reporter for more info]*

Q: Alright, in a SUPERMARKET TABLOID! [Responds, embarrassed]

Paul: YEAH, COME ON! Was this called the *National Enquirer* by any chance? I think you'll find it's on a par with "Aliens Turn My Son into an Olive," *[Reporters laugh]* which was a headline in Britain recently.

YO, SOLE-A-MEEE-YO! *[Sings in an operatic voice]* UH! *[Reporters yell out questions all at once]* It's getting tense. Wait a minute! *[Points]* You first!

Q: What do you think of scalpers making money off your tickets?

Paul: Unfortunately, that's a sign of where we live, you know. We live in the "Free West" and people are allowed to do that. You're allowed to buy a ticket and anyone will buy it for three times the value or more. I don't really like it because it's unfair to the fans, but we all know that. And this is nothing new. There's nothing I can do about . . . , so you know it's just tough. It's a fact of life really.

▲ This song had one of the most complicated lighting sequences—ranging from circle spots to laser grid patterns. "We Got Married," April 15, 1990, Joe Robbie Stadium, Miami, Florida.

▶ McCartney smiles and waves to the enthusiastic British crowd at Wembley Arena in Wembley Park, near London, England. During the London dates Prince Andrew, Bob Geldof, Cliff Richard, Elton John, Phil Collins, Peter Gabriel, Elvis Costello, Sting, George Martin, Donald Sutherland, Dick Lester, Bob Hoskins, and Cynthia Lennon attended the shows. January 14, 1990.

Q: Do you think the regular price of your tickets is too high?

Paul: I don't think so, no. This isn't the top price of the year, as tickets go.

Joe: Cheaper than Cher.

Paul: Pardon?

Joe: Cheaper than Cher.

Paul: CHEAPER THAN CHER! What do you want? AND I KEEP ME TROUSERS ON! *[Reporters laugh]* HEY, COME ON! Come ON guys! YOU KNOW WHAT I'M SAYING? NAAAH, you know. We try to price it at a nice kind of middle-of-the-road thing, so we're not too high and we're not too low.

Q: When's the last time you sat back after you wrote a song and said, "That is a hit"?

Paul: Hmm, I don't know. *[Someone yells, "Love Me Do"!]* LOVE ME DO? *[Reporters laugh]* No, NO! Ha, ha! We have some comedians amongst us today. Good! MIKE, I think it's YOUR turn. QUICK! NO! I don't know actually. *[Paul giggles]* Give him half a chance. I don't know, you know. I've been lucky enough to do that a lot in my life. I can't remember when the last time was.

Q: I understand you speak Spanish very well.

Paul: Not very well. I speak a little bit.

Q: Can you say something?

Paul: SHA-URE! *Naturalmente.* (Naturally.)

Q: Can you say in Spanish what are the most pressing environmental problems in our nation?

Paul: OH, BOY! *[Press laughs]* Well, listen, baby I'd love to . . . *[She interrupts him and begins to speak in Spanish]* Yeah, *sí.* Well, I mean, I'd love to be able to do that, but honestly, I don't know it that well . . . , however, what I do know in Spanish . . .

◀ Paul sings "Jet" at Wembley Arena, January 14, 1990, Wembley Park, England.

Q: Okay, tell me what you do know.

Paul: See, what they teach you in school is like real daft stuff that you can never use in your life except at *mad* press conferences like this . . . , *[She continues to talk while he's talking]* and I would like to now recite a poem, IF I MAY? PLEASE? *[She finally shuts up and reporters snicker]* Which is in SPANISH. We played Spain and I said my old teacher told me this is like a real famous Spanish folklore story 'cause no one had ever 'eard of it. But it goes like this: *[Speaks with an exaggerated Spanish accent]*

> *Tres conejos, en un árbol,*
> *tocando el tambor*
> *que sí, que no*
> *que sí, lo he visto yo.*

HEY! *[Reporters applaud]* THANK YOU SO MUCH! And now a word about the environment! You'll have to tell them about the environment, baby. . . . YOU'LL have to translate.

Q: What does the poem mean?

Paul: That means: three rabbits, in a tree, playing a drum. Why yes? Why no? Why yes? I have seen it. *[Laughs]*

Q: I've noticed at your concerts that there is an outpouring of love from your adoring fans. What do you think of these people who are just flipped out of their minds . . . ?

Paul: Well, I love it, you know. That's what we come here to do. . . . We come here to have a party and if everyone sort of sits down and doesn't party, then we're not that happy. So, it's great, you know. We're finding at these concerts . . . a lot of emotion. There's a lot of feeling out there. . . . So, it's great for us, really great when you see 'em. At a lot of the shows, during "Let It Be" they light lighters. . . . And you see the whole stadium there for this song, which is kind of a positive, hopeful, song. . . . It's really very gratifying. It's great actually. And then when they all go MAD and PARTY and DANCE around. I mean, that is what I'd do, if I were at the show. *[Thinks about what he just said]* I AM at the show! *[Reporters laugh]* If I were in the audience, I mean. *[Giggles]*

It's a pretty mixed audience that we get here now. It's not really so much just girls anymore. And I say . . . . If they're really shouting and partying and stuff, they paid their money, they can do just what they want, as far as I'm concerned. WE LOVE IT!

Okay guys, thank you! Ta, da . . . ! Okay guys, I REALLY GOTTA GO NOW! See ya guys. Take it easy. *[Waves goodbye and gets cornered by reporters as he tries to leave]*

At this point members of the media stormed the press table with a bout of Beatlemania, pleading with Paul to sign albums, CDs, and photos. One reporter even requested that Paul autograph the Hofner bass he had brought with him. The mayhem ensued for about three minutes, while Paul's entourage gracefully glided him out the door and back to his waiting wife and band.

—JOE JOHNSON (of the syndicated radio show *Beatle Brunch*)

I SAW HIM

December 11, 1989,
Madison Square
Garden, New York,
New York

Born in 1961, I was quite young when the Beatles happened. Yet I was very much aware of them (who could *not* be?) and bopped like any kid would to their songs. I remember watching the Beatles cartoons on television. Sometime in the mid-1960s I discovered my brother's Beatles albums and would sit in his room listening to them and gaze at Paul! I had a crush on him even then.

When I was older, I asked my brother some details about this beautiful man. Was he married? (Damn! He already was by then.) By the time I was old enough to buy my own records, the Beatles were breaking up! Why was I born too late? Grrrrr! In 1970 I proudly became a BEATLEMANIAC!

Anyway, by 1976 I was feeling totally deprived about my Beatles obsession (mostly Paul). I never had the chance to see any of them live until the Wings over America Tour. I was fifteen at the time, and my parents were certain that a McCartney concert would involve exposure to . . . *gasp* . . . DRUGS! No matter how much I begged, they would not allow me to attend the concert. I was totally crushed and hated my parents for years because of this.

Many years later, in 1989, I was a married woman with two young children. My husband had already tolerated my love of Paul for twelve years (we met in 1977) and that wonderful, loving man promised to take me to Paul's concert in New York City. I called incessantly for one and one-half hours from the moment the tickets went on sale at Madison Square Garden. With charge card in hand, I got through. Then the really cruel blow was dealt—both shows were sold-out! Aarrgghh!

McCartney raises the actual Hofner bass that was played during the last U.S. Beatles concert at San Francisco's Candlestick Park on August 29, 1966, in a salute to the crowd after "Get Back." July 29, 1990, Soldier Field, Chicago, Illinois.

"Get Back" performed July 29, 1990 at Chicago's Soldier Field to a sell-out crowd of 55,630.

I wept—then made the best move of my life by calling my cousin. Her husband "knew a man" who could get tickets for *anything*—at a price! "CALL HIM!" I pleaded. The tickets cost us $250 each, which was a small fortune for us in those days. The seats were located about center court, the first set of seats off the floor—not too shabby!

I cannot tell you what I was going through in the days leading up to the concert. Words do not describe the intense excitement and fear. I was so afraid that something would happen to prevent me from seeing Paul. Then I got the flu! Days before the concert, I was very ill and bedridden. "I *knew* it!" I cried. Miraculously, the day before the concert I was feeling better.

The night of the concert, I felt as though I would crawl out of my skin. When we finally left our hotel for "the Garden," traffic was intense with wall-to-wall cabs. Macca was the man of the night to be sure and I lamented out loud that we would never get there in time. My cousin's hubby nearly threw me out of the car, saying, "You can get out and WALK to the f*ing concert if the traffic doesn't start to move. . . . So, SHUT UP!"

We finally got in. Minutes passed so slowly, I thought I'd die. The preshow film with the Beatles started. It led us ever-so-slowly through the '60s and '70s. I was murmuring, "I want

Paul feigns fright at seeing a certain photographer in the Wembley photo pit. "Figure of Eight," January 14, 1990, Wembley Arena, Wembley Park, England.

now, I WANT NOW!" Ironically the screen shouted "N-O-W!" (*Did they hear me?* I wondered.) Then, as if by magic Paul strolled onto the stage. I thought my heart would burst! Suddenly I was in a trance and couldn't move. I couldn't believe that I was actually in the same building with this man, whom I had loved for so many years.

As Paul played one Beatles song after another, I became almost giddy with excitement. (No drugs, Mom!) Sitting back in my chair I screamed, "Oh, God, PLEASE, NO MORE!" Then he played "I Saw Her Standing There." Calming myself, I reasoned, "Ro, if you have a heart attack and die, you will never get a chance to tell your friends that you saw Macca!"

Another high point was "The Long and Winding Road," a favorite of mine. It always makes me cry, but I had promised myself that tonight there would be no crying. When Paul began to sing, I lost all control and wept—no, sobbed. My husband grew concerned and asked if I was alright. "Yes, I'm just so incredibly happy," was my reply. "Oh, okay then," he said as he patted my back.

When the show was over, I didn't want Paul to leave. I wanted him to come back onstage and do it all over again. We left with my ears still buzzing from the music. That concert trip to New York was my gift for the year, and the couple of photos I sneaked past the guards (who were standing right in front of me for most of the show, blast them!) got a place of honor on my fridge. When Valentine's Day came, I walked up to the fridge, looked at my favorite picture, and said, "Happy Valentine's Day, Ro!" I did the same on Mother's Day, our anniversary, and my birthday. What a memory—the thrill of that night has lingered still, and as I later told a friend, it definitely was the "most exciting night of my life." She thought my statement was absurd and asked, "What about your wedding day?" My answer: "Nawwwww!"

—ROSEMARIE "MARTHA" DIANESE

"Jet" at Wembley Arena. Paul glances out at the fourteen-thousand-plus crowd, many of whom came repeatedly to each of the eleven Wembley shows. Paul and Linda arrived in a helicopter that landed at Wembley Stadium, adjacent to the arena. A black Bentley filled with fresh flowers drove Paul and Linda the few blocks to the arena where the stars were greeted by waiting fans. January 14, 1990, Wembley Arena, Wembley Park, England.

I SAW HIM

November 23, 1989,
Forum, Inglewood,
California

I'd waited all my life to see Paul McCartney. And since he hardly ever toured, he'd taken on an almost mythical quality for me. I would always champion him to my friends, but to them he just seemed remote and past it. They seemed to think he was some sort of a fake. I had almost given up hope of ever seeing him when along came the 1989–90 world tour.

My boss wouldn't let me off for the show. So I quit my job and bought a ticket to Los Angeles. On Thanksgiving Day I wandered the grounds of the Forum, waiting for Paul's first stateside concert in thirteen years. A worker told me that the sound check was scheduled for about 4:30 P.M. so I made sure to be at the artists' entrance at that time. There were twelve other fans gathered there, eleven women and one other man. One of the women had also quit her job to come that day. The man had spent $850 to fly in from Alaska!

Excited but patient, we waited as 4:30 P.M. came and went. Finally, around 5:15, the limo arrived. Paul had the driver stop in front of us as he rolled down the window. Linda was on our side and gave us a big smile as she said, "How are you all doing?" Then Paul leaned across her and stuck his head out the window. The women swooned and rushed the car. I stood back and savored the moment as he shook hands and signed a few autographs. As I watched him skillfully handle the excited fans it suddenly hit me that he was for real. He thanked them for coming and seemed just as pleased to see them as they were to see him. I thought, *Yeah, there's the Big Guy! He's for real and he's really got it together, doesn't he?* Paul must have noticed me standing off to the side shaking my head because he looked at me and then raised his eyebrows as if to say "What's all this then?" He gave me the thumbs-up (which I returned), and signaled the driver to move on.

—CORRIN J. GREEN

◄ "Figure it out for yourself, little girl. . . ." An attentive look from Paul to this photographer. "Figure of Eight," January 14, 1990, Wembley Arena, Wembley Park, England.

► Paul dances in the dark during the instrumental part of "Coming Up." July 29, 1990, Soldier Field, Chicago, Illinois.

December 7, 1989,
Skydome, Toronto,
Ontario, Canada

I blame Toronto. Before Toronto I had admired the *Band on the Run* album, and, when pressed, would offer "Paul" in answer to that all-important question of who my favorite Beatle was. I owned, and had loved to bits, one Beatles album—a tape of *Sgt. Pepper's Lonely Hearts Club Band*, the rock album that had opened my ears to popular music. I liked the Beatles a lot, but was never a fan in the true sense of the word.

I made the trek up from London, Ontario (about two hours from Toronto), with a couple of Beatle-crazy friends. We had eighth-row tickets, and I remember that on the drive up my friend and I kept turning to each other and yelling "EIGHTH ROW!" and grinning in fits of covetousness.

We had printed out set lists before the concert, dutifully transcribed from fans in other parts of the world who had seen the shows. These lists were sent via the Internet to a newsgroup called "rec.music.beatles," where they were posted for all to see.

Knowing the set lists heightened my desire to read the Internet messages, which I found descriptive and thrilling. On the journey to Toronto these song lists created great anticipation about what Paul would play. I was now an enthusiastic participant, having primed myself for weeks by swapping McCartney audiotapes with people to fill in my musical gaps. In particular, I had listened often and with curiosity to a third-generation dub of Paul's then-new album called *Flowers in the Dirt.* It slowly grew on me, taking a firm hold.

The fact that I had managed to get through my life without ever hearing "Maybe I'm Amazed" was a topic of heated discussion during the trip. The cassette was unearthed and played for me on a Walkman in the back of the van. It had an intriguing melody, but most of all it featured a tremendous chord, which was its charm and mystery. I fell in love with it immediately. The second time I ever heard "Maybe I'm Amazed" was when Paul sang it—the memory still brings shivers to my spine.

The seats were fabulous—somehow unnervingly close in that great vastness of a stadium— and gave us a terrific view of the band. I had to keep reminding myself that, yes, that was Paul McCartney singing up there—right there! Even though we had a sneak preview of the songs from the set list, we kept turning to each other in disbelief with hopeful, sometimes imploring looks that said, "I can't believe he's actually going to play it!" We knew that this tour was the first time the title track from *Sgt. Pepper's Lonely Hearts Club Band* had ever been played live. The excitement was contagious and verged on the unbearable.

The most touching and moving experience for me was when the entire audience rose as one while Paul sang "Let It Be" and "Hey Jude." I stood on my seat and for one impulsive moment was captivated by the moving sea of candles behind me. The crowd hushed in anticipation and I felt suddenly alone, as if this experience was just for me—with all other eyes and ears directed forward. Impossibly bright and numerous, the flames swayed in silent, jubilant arrays, speaking a universal language of love and respect. I imagined what feelings this sight might have evoked from those onstage. My heart quivered. I turned around and rejoined the celebration, not noticing until much later that the candle my friend and I shared had dripped molten wax onto our hands. Ouch!

Paul waves his guitar in the air after "Yesterday," only to be outdone by some enterprising fans who lift their formerly attached chairs in a salute to their hero. July 29, 1990, Soldier Field, Chicago, Illinois.

One small but lovely detail I observed while looking back was the giant projections on the dome ceiling that recalled psychedelia in their swirling motions. I wondered what the special-effects people did when there was no ceiling. Someone must have worked very hard to achieve that effect. How many people actually looked at it?

We did go to the hotel where Paul was supposed to be staying, saw a line of white limos enter the garage, summoned our courage, and took the elevator to the penthouse floor. However, something stopped us from going in. We knew how much Paul values his privacy and when the doors opened, we peered out into the hallway and took the elevator back down. It wasn't fear, it was a matter of respect that still pleases me. I will never know if he actually was there, of course. But even so, it's a nice feeling of not knowing.

—MARK TOVEY

▲ A surprised and amused Paul looks at a group of preteen female fans screaming their lungs out. He later imitated them by screaming and pulling on his hair during "Ain't That a Shame." "Figure of Eight," December 5, 1989, Rosemont Horizon, Rosemont, Illinois.

◄ Sweat streams down Paul's face as he sings "Ooh, what she said" from "Jet." January 14, 1990, Wembley Arena, Wembley Park, England.

I SAW HIM

June 28, 1990, King's Dock Arena, Liverpool, England

I went to see Paul in Liverpool with a tour arranged through one of the American Beatles fanzines. Since I was traveling alone, this brought me in touch with a group of people who loved Paul as much as I did and I developed some long-term friendships. When we pulled up to the Moat House Hotel, the marquee said, "Welcome American Beatles Fans." Paul's band and entourage were also staying at this very hotel.

Part of the trip included a tour of Liverpool, where we were informed by our guide that Paul would be landing at Speke Airport shortly. With no time to waste we hurried to the airport and waited for Paul to arrive.

When the plane landed the door opened and there was THE MAN himself—Paul McCartney! He was ushered into the waiting car and gave us a thumbs-up out of the rear window as I aimed my camera and clicked the shutter. I'm not much of a photographer, which was apparent after the picture was developed. It captured the excitement of the moment, but Paul can barely be seen.

Later, after the exhilaration of seeing Paul at the airport, a friend and I walked along the waterfront, where the stage and arena were being built. Paul was doing the sound check and we heard him play "Birthday"! What a surprise—especially since it wasn't added to the set list until the next show. Even Liverpudlians were getting a thrill out of this one. My friend started crying because it was her birthday.

That afternoon, after we got ready to go to the concert, I went to the hotel lobby. There on a cart, unattended, were Paul's stage clothes. His jacket had a liver bird (the city's symbol) appliqué sewn on it—specially for the Liverpool show. When the fans realized whose clothes they were, chaos ensued and a McCartney staffer had to rescue them before they became shredded souvenirs.

At the concert Americans had reserved seats on both sides of the stage, but the better places were in an open field next to the front of the stage. People had been drinking and drugging in line for hours. The first-aid area was just beneath our seats and they would frequently pass ailing fans on stretchers up and over the crowd. We saw many people end their concert experience that way.

One of the highlights of the show was Paul's emotional rendition of "Strawberry Fields/Help!/Give Peace a Chance"—a new medley dedicated to John. It was the first time Paul performed these songs on the tour, making it very special. When Paul tried to end "Give Peace a Chance," the crowd of fifty thousand continued to sing, compelling Paul to continue the song. It was an impassioned moment for Paul as he led the audience through several more choruses.

After the show, my new friends and I agreed that it was a beautiful Liverpool night—sitting outside listening to Paul McCartney.

—LINDA M. ROBBINS

◀ "Let It Be Liverpool" souvenir ticket jacket, which was given out with the tickets at the June 28, 1990, Liverpool concert at the King's Dock Arena, Liverpool, England.

▶ Paul smiles at Robbie and Hamish as he ends the jam during "Golden Slumbers/Carry That Weight/The End." February 14, 1990, Market Square Arena, Indianapolis, Indiana.

Paul and Hamish prepare to kick up their heels in unison to the pounding rhythm of "Get Back." July 29, 1990, Soldier Field, Chicago, Illinois.

I SAW HIM

April 20 and 21, 1990,
Maracana Stadium,
Rio de Janeiro, Brazil

Paul's concerts in Rio de Janeiro were an adventure for me and my friends. As soon as we knew Paul was coming to South America, I got crazy and didn't care how far I needed to travel. It didn't matter that I would need lots of money for tickets and bus fare. This would be the first time Paul would be playing in South America and I had to see him.

In 1990 I was absolutely bankrupt. I planned to sell my television and audio equipment, but at the last moment a helping hand reached out and gave me what I needed—money. The next morning I left for Brazil via bus with friends and after two days of traveling we arrived in Rio de Janeiro in the middle of a torrential rain. To our disappointment Paul's concert was postponed. Since we didn't have any tickets, we left our luggage in the apartment and went to buy them. After that, our next stop was the Rio Palace Hotel—where Paul, Linda, and the band members were staying. With no concert that night we could wait at the hotel and hope to see Paul.

When we arrived, there were hundreds of fans waiting outside in the rain. They screamed and sang his songs. Many came from Argentina, as I had. Suddenly, he walked onto the balcony of his eighth-floor room to wave to the crowd. We all went crazy. It was like Beatlemania all over again! He wore a Brazilian soccer team T-shirt and came out several times to wave and shout to us. It was an exciting moment for me since this was the first time I was so close to him. (So close, yet so far away at the same time.)

◀ "Whoa yea-ah. Whoa-oh, yea-ah. Whoa-whoa-whoa-WHOA, yeah. Whoa, whoa-whoa-whoa, YEAH!" Paul's introduction to "Get Back," December 4, 1989, Rosemont Horizon, Rosemont, Illinois.

▼ Paul eyes an enthusiastic fan. "My Brave Face," December 3, 1989, Rosemont Horizon, Rosemont, Illinois. At this show the film was not shown due to a technical problem. Paul casually walked out on stage unannounced. After the first couple of songs he apologized for the projector "being busted" and commented on the physical condition of his drummer, Chris Whitten, who had noticeable facial bruises. "He's smashed his face cycling."

"Things We Said Today," December 4, 1989, Rosemont Horizon, Rosemont, Illinois. The day after the last show Paul took his family to see *Back to the Future* at a Chicago theater. He was recognized by one lucky fan.

My friend and I decided that it just wasn't enough for us to see the concerts, so we planned to get into the preshow press conference being held at the stadium on April 20. Our plan was to pose as journalists with a pair of fake press ID cards we made by hand in Buenos Aires. Unfortunately, we weren't allowed into the press conference, but we did get a photo pass—which would allow us to be much closer to the stage than I would have been with my regular tickets.

The rain didn't stop and two hours before show time I could see thousands of people getting wet inside the stadium. In spite of the bad weather, it was like a dream for me. I couldn't believe that I would be standing so close to Paul in the middle of that big stadium filled with more than a hundred thousand people.

When the opening film started it was one of the most exciting moments in my life. There I was in front of the stage—standing shoulder to shoulder with the *real* photographers. It was funny because I was pretending to be a professional photographer, but all I had was a red pocket camera. Everyone was looking at me, thinking *Who the hell is this guy?* Finally my childhood dream—to see the man I idolized perform his songs—was becoming a reality. I had only seen Paul in photos or films. So now the legend was alive and standing just nine feet away from me. It was a magical moment because just as Paul stepped onto the stage, the rain that had been showering Rio for almost a week suddenly stopped.

One of the show's highlights was Paul's new rendition of the rewritten "P.S. I Love You" and "Love Me Do" medley. It was a revelation for me to see Paul singing with just a microphone in his hand as he danced around the stage. The show was great and when Paul spoke in Portuguese to the audience about saving the planet the crowd cheered him on.

The following day's show was sold-out and Paul played before a record-breaking audience of 184,368. He was later honored by the *Guinness Book of World Records* for the largest audience attendance for a solo artist at one concert. I was proud to be part of that historical event.

Paul seemed in a happier mood now that the skies had totally cleared up. It was the first time I saw Paul onstage performing songs such as "Sgt. Pepper's Lonely Hearts Club Band," "Hey Jude," "Golden Slumbers/Carry That Weight/The End," and many others. I thought, *I'm living one of the greatest and most beautiful dreams in my whole life!*

Paul thanks the Chicago audience and begins the opening chords to the last song, "Golden Slumbers/Carry That Weight/The End." July 29, 1990, Soldier Field, Chicago, Illinois.

The next morning, I went with my friends to the Rio Palace Hotel in hopes of seeing Paul one more time. He came out on the balcony in the late afternoon with Linda and threw flowers to the fans below. In the confusion that followed, I grabbed one of those treasured souvenirs. Soon afterward, Paul, Linda, and the band left for the airport, slipping out the back way to avoid the hysteria but instead wound up in the middle of it. I was so close to him that I almost could touch him. He and the band waved to the fans as the bus drove away. I ran as fast as I could after it until I couldn't run anymore.

Those were magical and incredible days that I'll never forget as long as I live.

—JAVIER ESTRACH

February 9, 1990,
Worcester-Centrum,
Worcester, Massachusetts

On our way to the Worcester-Centrum, I had high hopes of seeing Paul McCartney in person. My husband, Bob, knew how anxious I was to see the concert and meet Paul. He teased me all day with faux sightings—like at the restaurant we went to before the show when Bob quietly said, "You're not going to believe who just walked in!" I let him know that I'm not that easily fooled and, if Paul was around, I'd know it.

From the restaurant we walked toward the concert site to a busy intersection and waited for the light to change. My usually quiet husband started to jump around and scream, "Oh my god, Diane! Look . . . IT'S PAUL!" I glanced up at him and said, nonchalantly, "Yeah, right, Bob." Then I looked where he was looking and to my shock I saw Paul and Linda in a limo! The windows were down and Paul was staring at us and giving Bob the thumbs-up. I couldn't believe my eyes and slipped off the curve, falling over. My husband caught me just in time. I looked up and Paul and Linda were laughing at me! Then they both gave us the thumbs-up and waved as the limo drove off.

—DIANE HARRINGTON

Recognition to the photographer during "Coming Up." July 29, 1990, Soldier Field, Chicago, Illinois.

I SAW HIM

July 24 and 25, 1990,
Sullivan Stadium, Foxboro,
Massachusetts, filming of
Get Back

On July 24, I began the four-hour drive to Foxboro with my friends Sue and Connie. In my car windows were signs that read "Paul McCartney Concert or Bust!" It brought us a steady stream of horn toots and thumbs-up from passersby.

We lingered at the stadium with fans who revealed juicy news items such as the fact that Paul would be arriving soon by helicopter. They insisted on including us—total strangers—in their group photo, merely because we were also devoted McCartney fans. This was our first taste of the incredibly warm, family feeling that permeated the entire concert scene. It was the kind of place you could drop off your ten-year-old kid for the evening and know that he or she would be perfectly safe. Conversations flowed naturally among strangers, for we were all united in the common bond of love for this man and his music.

Later we returned to the stadium just in time to hear Paul's sound check as he warmed up with "C Moon." That's when it really hit me that he was there and I was finally going to see him. We longed to be inside and witness this private performance.

At the gate, we were handed blue flyers by a man who walked briskly by. The flyer read: "You are invited to participate in the filming of the Paul McCartney World Tour at Foxboro Stadium tomorrow." We could hardly believe our good fortune. So this was why there was a free night scheduled between the Tuesday and Thursday concerts.

As soon as the gates opened we proceeded past three rows of security men, who checked our possessions carefully. Our excitement grew as we neared the stage. One of the ushers said our binoculars would not be necessary because we were in the "gold seats." Not only were they gold, but they were in the *second row!*

▶ The blue flyer that was handed out at the first Foxboro concert (July 24, 1990), announcing the filming of *Get Back* on the following day.

◀ Camera crews were filming every night at Wembley Arena for the concert video of the tour, called *Get Back*. Film crews followed the tour and many cities were filmed. Fans from different parts of the world were picked to profile in the video. The soundtrack of one of the Philadelphia shows (July 14 and 15, 1990, Veterans Stadium) was used for the video and a concert was staged at Sullivan Stadium in Foxboro, Massachusetts, on July 25 to fill in footage they needed to complete the documentary. "Jet," January 14, 1990, Wembley Arena, Wembley Park, England.

YOU ARE INVITED TO PARTICIPATE IN THE FILMING OF THE PAUL MCCARTNEY WORLD TOUR AT FOXBORO STADIUM, FOXBORO, MA., TOMORROW, JULY 25, 1990 FROM 7:30 PM - 9:30 PM.

BRING THIS INVITATION TO GATE W1.
ADMISSION GUARANTEED TO THE FIRST 1,000.

When Paul finally appeared my eyes followed him everywhere, not wanting to lose a second in which I could "feast" on this gorgeous man. As far as I was concerned, there was no one else in that stadium except Paul and me. This was as close to pure joy as I've ever felt—and the thought of seeing him the following day was the icing on the cake!

The next morning we drove over to the stadium to find out what we could about the filming of the movie. When we produced our blue flyers, pink wristbands were placed on our arms and became our entrance tickets. (I didn't take my bracelet off until after Paul closed his tour in Chicago, four days later.)

All day we "talked, ate, and breathed" the concert, in anticipation of seeing him again. At 7:00 P.M. we entered the stadium to learn that out of the forty-five thousand people present at the previous night's concert, only one thousand lucky people would be participating in the filming of tonight's free concert. As we were herded toward our seats, a Hollywood movie crew set up lighting, cameras, and stand-ins. The director was running around with his megaphone, giving everyone orders. He directed us to be very quiet between musical numbers, but to "make like an audience and scream like hell when Paul sings"—something we proved to be innately talented at doing. We were told the sound track had already been recorded at the Philadelphia concert and only visuals would be taped in Foxboro. While waiting, we filled out forms that waived our right to sue Paul McCartney for being extras in his movie. "Are you kidding?" we joked. "We'd have gladly *paid* to be in this movie!" From above a helicopter swooped dramatically over the side of the stadium and the crowd began to cheer. We knew it was him!

After about two hours, Paul finally appeared. (It's true what they say about the interminable waiting around when movies are being made.) What followed was an informal glimpse of Paul-the-man, as opposed to Paul-the-polished-performer, whom we had seen the night before. For three hours the band mimed a dozen songs for the cameras with a ten-minute wait between songs. These pauses were the highlight of the evening for me, perhaps because I've always enjoyed Paul's personality and sense of humor as much as his music.

Paul could have sat down and waited, like the rest of us, but he took it upon himself to keep us amused. He sang a little Scottish song a cappella, joked with the audience and played soft chords as he walked slowly around the stage, watching his guitar, not the crowd. We stared, mesmerized. Was he composing? I heard a little jazz and a little rock. It was done beautifully. Only once did I recognize the chords he was playing and the crowd began singing "She's a Woman." Sometimes another band member would join in and an impromptu jam session followed.

I got the impression that Paul could not hold his guitar without playing it. There was no way he could just sit and wait when he could be making music instead. My eyes were riveted to the stage, not wanting to miss anything he might say, play, sing, or do to entertain us.

During one quiet moment, a brave soul in the audience started to softly sing:

"We love you, Paul, oh yes we do,
We don't love anyone as much as you,
When you're not near us, we're blue,
Oh, Paul, we love you."

And the crowd joined in for this tribute, which I had not heard since the Beatlemania days.

"Figure of Eight," December 5, 1989, Rosemont Horizon, Rosemont, Illinois. Toward the end of this show a fan threw a Paul doll onstage. McCartney picked it up and pretended to be a ventriloquist, holding the doll up to the microphone and talking in a high-pitched voice. He placed his effigy on a nearby amplifier, occasionally scolding it to the audience's delight.

Paul hammed it up continually during takes, missing cues and laughing about it. He played Robbie's guitar part instead of his own and even waved his hands in the air when he was supposed to be "playing" his guitar. His cute-and-crazy charm—which first endeared him (and the other Beatles) to fans back in 1964—is still very much intact.

The funniest moment came after the attempted taping of "Coming Up," when the sound track was not coming across at the correct speed. As we waited for it to be fixed, Paul began to mimic the sound track and sang "Coming Up" in a fast high-pitched voice similar to a 33 rpm record played at 45 rpm. He walked and played with little jerky movements and the whole band joined in. Then he began the song again at a very slow speed (like a 45 record played at 33 rpm), moving in slow motion. It was hysterically funny because it was extremely accurate. I thought, *This man is such a genius he can even play his songs at different speeds and sound authentic!*

Always the gentleman, Paul thanked and applauded us for coming. We all went home that night feeling we'd been given a special gift—an inside look at the unrehearsed brilliance of this superstar.

—MARGO GRAHAM

Fans at many of the shows did the "swan dance" during this number, copying hand movements from McCartney's U.K. video of the song. "This One" December 4, 1989, Rosemont Horizon, Rosemont, Illinois.

I SAW HIM

November 2, 1989,
Palacio de los Deportes,
Madrid, Spain

During the show, Paul recited a Spanish poem he learned as a child in school. It was about three rabbits in a tree and Paul said:

Tres conejos, en un árbol,
tocando el tambor
que sí, que no
que sí, lo he visto yo.

The fans loved the effort Paul made to break the language barrier by speaking in Spanish whenever he could. He loved to interact with the crowd and at one point asked us to repeat everything he said: "Everyone say after me. Say, OH YEAH! *[Audience echoes phrase]* Say, Aw-RIGHT! *[Audience repeats phrase]* Say, Ooo-Kay! *[Audience repeats again]* Say, MALASALA-moe-CHUNA, WENAMA-cha-HEENEE, WAL-A-WASALA-moonday, classaka-POONdee!"

Since most people could not understand English, we were left completely dumbfounded by that last phrase, thinking it might have been something in English. Paul waited for our reaction, which left a surprising silence among the people in the crowd—who shrugged their shoulders with questioning looks. Then we realized the joke! Everyone broke into fits of laughter. It was incredibly funny and Paul found it most amusing as he jokingly said, "Very close!"

—Eufemiano S. Amillategui

Paul leans on band mate Robbie McIntosh, who plays an inspiring guitar solo on "Can't Buy Me Love." February 14, 1990, Market Square Arena, Indianapolis, Indiana.

I SAW HIM

During Paul's 1990 Japan tour, I stayed at the Okura Hotel in Tokyo in a reserved room right under Paul's penthouse floor. I canceled all my acting jobs during his stay because I couldn't concentrate on anything, knowing Paul was in town. This meant that my scheduled dramas, movies, and even my concert had to be canceled. Nothing was more important than meeting Paul.

At the hotel I thought about waiting for Paul in hopes of meeting him. He had to walk through the lobby to the swimming pool and some fans, posing as hotel guests, had already been successful at meeting him there. I just didn't have enough courage to do this, so I decided to stay in my room. Outside I could hear fans screaming for Paul and imagined that he was either leaving or coming back from somewhere.

I received a call from my agent who said, "Listen, Toko, you have to calm down because you might get an interview with Paul. . . ." "Oh, JESUS!" I screamed. But she continued, ". . . listen, don't get crazy, okay? It all depends on Paul's schedule. We can't tell when it's going to happen and Paul doesn't want to meet a hysterical interviewer, understand?" She knew how long I had loved and admired Paul. This would be the opportunity of a lifetime and I had to keep my cool somehow and not let my emotions take over.

The interview was to take place backstage at the Tokyo Dome just before his concert. Fuji Television would be videotaping my every move for a program called *Ohayoh Nice Day.* (Good Morning, Nice Day)

I was asked by the TV crews to say hello to Paul when he left the hotel to go to the concert. I told them that I needed that moment to be private, since it would be my first contact with Paul and I had to formally introduce myself and let him know about the interview. They had some reservations about it, but finally agreed.

Paul came out of the hotel smiling and waving to the fans. When I saw him I couldn't believe that he was REAL! The cameras were rolling, but I couldn't say anything! I wanted to treasure that moment for myself. Paul got into his limo and drove away.

We followed him in our van and caught up to his car. He was wearing sunglasses and was sitting next to Linda, who took some photos. The video director asked me to talk to him. I tried to open the window, but was unfamiliar with the mechanism that moved it. As I struggled, Paul smiled and waved to our camera. "Hello! How are ya?" he shouted. I finally slid the window open and in a weak, shaky voice said, "Paul, I'm going to interview you today!" He said, "Oh good, but you'll have to CONTROL YOURSELF!" At that moment I almost cried. He had talked to *me!* We had talked to each other! "See ya later. Okay?" he said as the limo drove off. I waved to him and the tears began to fall.

Backstage I waited patiently in the interview room, clutching flowers for Paul, plus a selection of my own CDs, felt badges that I embroidered with his and the band's names on them, some message cards, and my list of questions to ask. I was so nervous I could feel the sweat permeating my hands. Then Paul walked into the room, pointing and smiling at me. He put his palms together (in a praying gesture), bowed and said, "*Konichiwa!*" (Hello!) I greeted him back with, "*Konichiwa!*" and bowed. As I stood up he kissed me on the cheek and I cried, "NO!" He stepped back, surprised, and said, "Oh, no?" I wanted to explain my reaction, but was unable to because of the kiss. I just froze. He started to chant in fake Japanese, "*Hai-YAA! Humm-wo, jo-jo-JO. OOH, HAI!*" to make me laugh and ease my nervousness. I gained my composure and began the interview.

McCartney exudes confidence and sex appeal in this very atmospheric concert opener from the *Flowers in the Dirt* album. "Figure of Eight," January 14, 1990, Wembley Arena, Wembley Park, England.

Toko: Paul, what do you usually do with your free time at home when you're not writing songs, painting, or riding?

Paul: When I'm not doing that? *[I nod]* . . . 'Cause that's what I'm doing most of the time while I'm there. Hmm . . . *[Thinks about it as he looks up at the ceiling]* Eating, sleeping, waking up. That's very important, the waking up bit. *[Smiles]* And, yeah, I like to horse ride. . . . We have sheep you know, and when they need to come in for a clipping or something, Linda and I ride around and round them up like cowboys. . . . So we like that. I like walking. . . .

Toko: Walk down the street like an ordinary person?

Paul: On the farm I like to go into the woods and clear a path and make a fire. Very simple things I like because most of my life is involved with very complicated things. . . . I need the balance. So complex things: high-tech cameras, microphones, and recording studios. . . . It's nice for me to get balance. I often go out and if the woods are thick, they say to me, "Go make a path!" Yee-ss SIR! *[Salutes with his right hand and pretends to chop trees, making a chopping noise]*

Toko: You do that?

Paul: Yeah!

Toko: Ordinary life?

Paul: Yeah, when I have a day off. That's what I like to do. It's just nice for me. Very relaxing . . . and I like painting, as you mentioned.

Toko: Do you paint a lot?

Paul: I started painting seriously in 1983 and it's good. I like painting. The canvas is bigger and bigger as I get more comfortable. *[Pretends he's painting on an imaginary canvas]* OILS! *[Makes the noise of the brush on canvas] Shaah! Shaah!*

Toko: Do you draw a picture of things or people?

Paul: Depends. Sometimes I paint a portrait of Linda. I paint quite a lot of her. She's the only one who sits still. The kids won't sit. And I paint abstracts as well . . . just colors . . . BIG abstracts. I like it. It's good for me.

The interview lasted more than thirty minutes and at the end, Paul held out his hand to shake mine. I quickly tried to wipe the sweat off first and he said to me gently, "No, no, it's good. We can do this." And we shook. I gave him my gifts and he politely said, "*Domo!*" (Thank you!) Paul examined my CD "The Woman in Me" and asked, "Do you write songs?" I shook my head to indicate "no." He looked again at the CD and said, "Your shoulder's shining" (referring to the strapless dress I wore on the cover). I began to sob and Paul said, "No crying! Big girls don't cry!"

He was perfect, just as I expected him to be. We said our good-byes and I thought later that I should have stayed and talked to him more. It might seem ridiculous, but I felt as if he was an old friend; he was so easy to talk to. I had another chance years later to talk to him during his 1993 tour and he was just as wonderful, but that's another story.

—Tomoko Fujita

◀ Paul introduces the last song of the show, "Golden Slumbers/Carry That Weight/The End." At the end of this concert a fan handed Paul a Hofner bass to sign. Another offered Paul *Back to the Future* sunglasses, which he and Linda put on for a laugh. December 4, 1989, Rosemont Horizon, Rosemont, Illinois.

▶ McCartney belts out "Jet" at the Rosemont Horizon, December 5, 1989, Rosemont, Illinois. Roger Daltrey was in the audience.

▲ "Rough Ride," January 9, 1990,
NEC Birmingham, England.

I SAW HIM

In Chicago there was to be a press conference before the show and my wife, Kathi, and I made every attempt to find the right people who could get us in. Details were sketchy and there was no commitment on their part. "At least we're going to the concert," Kathi said, trying to console herself. But then the phone rang with instructions to get to Soldier Field right away. We were in! Dashing down the stairs, we grabbed a cab and told him to "FLOOR IT to the stadium!"

Upon arriving, we were confused as to the meeting place, which was complicated by the fact that Paul's plane was delayed by a thunderstorm. We finally found out where to go and were escorted down a ramp that was used by limos to enter the backstage area. Most of the people who had gone down this ramp earlier were "parked" alongside of it. Fortunately, our guide took us past this group of photojournalists and deposited us in the backstage tent where the press conference was to be held.

There were rows of chairs for about seventy-five people and food—vegetarian hors d'oeuvres and pizzas—was served. Press kits filled with bios and pictures were on the chairs. Paul, Linda, and the band members stopped and posed for pictures just outside the tent. Then Paul came in by himself and held a press conference. It was an indescribable feeling to be in the same room with Paul for something other than a concert. I did not ask any questions, but I did take a few notes:

Paul: *[Singing in an operatic voice as he enters the room]* O, SOLE, MIO. Hello! How are ya doing? Alright? YO! Alright, let's go CHI-CA-GO! *[Raises fist in the air]* Soldier Field! Okay! *[Reporters start to cheer]* Calm down. Now calm down, please.

Q: What do you like to do in Chicago?

Paul: What do I like to do? Sit around and talk to people of the press. This is one of my favorite things. *[Grins and sips from a coffee mug]*

Q: I was wondering, what is your place with all the dance music?

Paul: I like a lot of modern music. You know, I think it's good. I like dance music. Umm, it's not particularly what I do, you know, and radio over here puts me in like sort of *[Wide-eyed, he raises his eyebrows, rocks his head from side to side, then winks]* Aaa-DULT Con-TEMP-o-rary. *[All the reporters start to talk at once]*

Paul: JUBBA-JUBBA-KNOWA-WATCHA-MEANA! *[Mimics them talking at once]*

Q: Why did you pick Chicago for the last show?

Paul: I don't know really. The promoter or somebody said, "Would you like to come back to Chicago?" We had a few options of where to finish the tour and this was the most exciting. I always liked Chicago. It's one of my cities, you know. *[Reporter yells his approval and Paul responds, pointing to him]* HEY, Man! I'm telling YOU!

◀ The famous dueling jam between Paul, Hamish, and Robbie during the grand finale song, "Golden Slumbers/Carry That Weight/The End." July 29, 1990, Soldier Field, Chicago, Illinois.

"BOY, you're gonna carry that weight . . . ," sing Paul and Linda in unison. "Golden Slumbers/Carry That Weight/The End," July 29, 1990, Soldier Field, Chicago, Illinois.

Q: Thank you, Paul, for your work in helping to spread the word about saving the environment. What can people do to help save the planet?

Paul: Thank you for thanking me. It's great. Especially from the young studs here. Umm . . . *[Reporter tries to interrupt and Paul yells at him]* SHUT UP! I'm talking to 'er. See these older people they just don't understand. DO YOU MIND? What was the actual question?

   If you think about joining things like Friends of the Earth or Greenpeace or PETA—any of these organizations—they're very good at telling you what you can do. . . . Just believe, that's the main thing. Believe the world needs saving and you'll save it.

Q: What would you have chosen for a career if you hadn't gone into rock 'n' roll?

Paul: I think the nearest thing I could ever think to do was like to be a teacher, 'cause that's where I was heading. I don't think I would have been a very good one. *[Laughs]* So you know, THANK GOD for ROCK 'N' ROLL!

Q: Don't you think your stand on the environment tends to be political at these concerts?

Paul: I never really meant to be kind of political. My main thing is just to be a musician. But in 1989, when we started this tour, this big hole appeared over the Antarctic—a fifty-mile hole. . . . It worries people.

   Normally at these conferences I'll ask anyone who's *not* worried about the future of the earth and the ecology to put their hands up, please. *[Pauses to check out the audience for*

hands and sees a reporter raise his hand] Go ahead then, SMART ASS! *[Taunts reporter]*
What are you gonna say? *[Embarrassed, reporter puts down his hand]* No, he's just
joking. . . .

All I'm doing is giving publicity to that cause and I think it is a very good cause. . . .
With the help of these young people we're gonna turn it 'round. . . . Sorry, got to go!

Time passed all too quickly and the conference was over. Some people stopped Paul for
autographs as he left the tent. I took some pictures at the end with a camera hidden in a "secure
area" of my shorts!

It was a warm, humid, July night and we walked back (on air!) to our hotel after the concert,
fervently hoping the future would hold more Macca concerts for us.

LARRY GOODMAN

A rare photograph of the McCartneys
kissing backstage as Linda bids Paul
farewell on her way to the dressing
room. Paul proceeded to the press
tent where seventy-five members of
the media fired questions at him. July
29, 1990, Soldier Field, Chicago,
Illinois.

McCartney holds a Van Gogh book, a present from a guest, and poses with an enthusiastic Linda by a replica of Maracana Stadium (Rio de Janeiro, Brazil). Paul played for 184,368 people there on April 21, 1990, breaking Frank Sinatra's attendance record and earning Paul a prestigious Guinness Award, which was presented at the party. December 12, 1990, End of the World Tour Party, Boardwalk Restaurant, Soho, London, England.

1991 CONCERT DATES

1991 SECRET GIGS—EUROPE May 8: Zeleste Club, Barcelona, Spain • May 10: Mean Fiddler, Harlesden, England • June 5: Teatro Tendo, Naples, Italy • June 7: St. Austell Coliseum, St. Austell, England • July 19: Southend Cliffs Pavilion, Westcliff-on-Sea, England • July 24: Falkoner Theatre, Copenhagen, Denmark

Paul talks to a guest at the End of the World Tour Party before dinner. The dinner was a buffet of Linda McCartney's vegetarian delicacies prepared by tour caterers, Eat Your Hearts Out. December 12, 1990, Boardwalk Restaurant, Soho, London, England.

THE NEW WORLD TOUR
1993 CONCERT DATES

PAUL McCARTNEY
THE NEW WORLD TOUR
LOS ANGELES
ANAHEIM STADIUM
SATURDAY 17TH APRIL 1993
THE LIPA TICKET

1993 EUROPE (REHEARSALS) February 5: Docklands, London, England • February 18, 19: Forum, Assago, Milan, Italy • February 22, 23: Festhalle, Frankfurt, Germany

1993 AUSTRALIA/NEW ZEALAND March 5: The Subiaco Oval, Perth, Australia • March 9, 10: Melbourne Cricket Ground, Melbourne, Australia • March 13: The Oval, Adelaide, Australia • March 16, 17, 20: Sydney Entertainment Centre, Sydney, Australia • March 22, 23: Parramatta Stadium, Parramatta, Australia • March 27: Western Springs Stadium, Auckland, New Zealand

1993 USA/CANADA April 14: Sam Boyd Silver Bowl, Las Vegas, Nevada • April 16: Hollywood Bowl Earth Day Concert, Hollywood, California • April 17: Anaheim Stadium, Anaheim, California • April 20: Aggie Memorial Stadium, Las Cruces, New Mexico • April 22: Astrodome, Houston, Texas • April 24: Louisiana Superdome, New Orleans, Louisiana • April 27: Liberty Bowl Memorial Stadium, Memphis, Tennessee • April 29: Busch Memorial Stadium, St. Louis, Missouri • May 1: Georgia Dome, Atlanta, Georgia • May 5: Riverfront Stadium, Cincinnati, Ohio • May 7: Williams-Brice Stadium, Columbia, South Carolina • May 9: Florida Citrus Bowl, Orlando, Florida • May 21: Winnipeg Stadium, Winnipeg, Canada • May 23: HHH Metrodome, Minneapolis, Minnesota • May 26: Folsom Field, Boulder, Colorado • May 29: Alamodome, San Antonio, Texas • May 31: Arrowhead Stadium, Kansas City, Missouri • June 2: Milwaukee County Stadium, Milwaukee, Wisconsin • June 4: Pontiac Silverdome, Pontiac, Michigan • June 6: Toronto Exhibition Stadium, Toronto, Canada • June 11: Giants Stadium, East

Concerts For the Environment
1993 EARTH DAY CONCERTS
HOLLYWOOD BOWL ● APRIL 16, 1993

PRINTED ON GRIDBOARD™ PANEL - 100 PERCENT POST CONSUMER RECYCLED FIBER MADE FROM OLD CORRUGATED CONTAINERS & DONATED BY GRIDCORE SYSTEMS INTERNATIONAL 5963 LA PLACE COURT #207 CARLSBAD, CA 92008 ● 619.431.8494

Rutherford, New Jersey • June 13: Veterans Stadium, Philadelphia, Pennsylvania • June 15: Blockbuster Pavilion, Charlotte, North Carolina **1993 EUROPE** September 3: Waldbühne, Berlin, Germany • September 5, 6: Stadhalle, Vienna, Austria • September 9: Olympiahalle, Munich, Germany • September 11, 14, 15: Earls Court, London, England • September 18, 19, 21: Westfalenhalle, Dortmund, Germany • September 23: H M Schleyer-Halle, Stuttgart, Germany • September 25: Scandinavium Hall, Göteborg, Sweden • September 27, 28: Oslo Spektrum, Oslo, Norway • October 1: Stockholm Globen Arena, Stockholm, Sweden • October 3: Maimarkthalle, Mannheim, Germany • October 5: H M Schleyer-Halle, Stuttgart, Germany • October 6: Festhalle, Frankfurt, Germany • October 9, 10: Ahoy Sportpaleis, Rotterdam, The Netherlands •

October 13, 14: Palais Omnisports de Bercy, Paris, France • October 17: Flanders Expo, Ghent, Belgium • October 20: Zenith, Toulon,

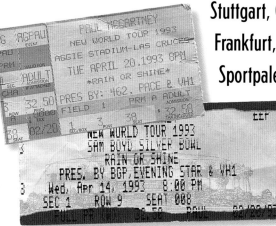

France • October 22, 23: Palasport, Florence, Italy • October 26, 27: Palau San Jordi, Barcelona, Spain **1993 JAPAN** November 12, 14, 15: Tokyo Dome, Tokyo, Japan • November 18, 19: Fukuoka Dome, Fukuoka, Japan **1993 MEXICO AND SOUTH AMERICA** November 25, 27: Autódromo Hermanos Rodriguez, Mexico City, Mexico • December 3: Pacaembu Stadium, São Paulo, Brazil • December 5: Paulo Leminski Rock, Curitiba, Brazil • December 10, 11, 12: Estadio River Plate, Buenos Aires, Argentina • December 16: Estadio Naçional, Santiago, Chile

▲ The indescribable "Macca Dance." "Coming Up," June 2, 1993, Milwaukee County Stadium, Milwaukee, Wisconsin.

▶ Earls Court, London, England, September 1993.

1993 The New World Tour

I
N MARCH OF 1993, two years and seven months after his most successful tour (The Paul McCartney World Tour) ended, McCartney began his third world tour, The New World Tour. As in previous tours, there was an album to promote, *Off the Ground* (1993), along with McCartney's massive catalog of hits to perform. A tour of this proportion following so close on the heels of another major tour resulted in a smaller percentage of sellouts in the United States, with only fourteen shows out of twenty-one considered sellouts. McCartney's concerts were performed in huge outdoor stadiums, some holding fifty thousand plus seats. In Europe, smaller venues of eighteen thousand or fewer were filled to capacity.

Nevertheless, McCartney's New World Tour broke records in ticket sales. In February of 1993, twenty thousand tickets were sold in eight minutes for McCartney's two concerts in Sydney, Australia, at the Sydney Entertainment Centre—a new world record. During the first four months of the seven-month tour, McCartney covered four countries, eighteen states, thirty-three shows, with a total attendance of 1.2 million. *Performance Magazine* ranked McCartney's tour second in gross sales, with twenty-one U.S. shows, bringing in $32,300,000—averaging $1,345,833 per show. Two shows in Mexico City grossed $6,564,416—a surprisingly high figure for an economically poor country. In Winnipeg, Canada, forty-one thousand seats were sold, breaking a ten-year-old state attendance record held by rocker David Bowie. At Milwaukee County Stadium, in spite of a continuous downpour of rain, attendance was at forty-nine thousand—more than for any World Series game in that park.

A concert tour of this magnitude needed three separate stages, requiring four traveling crews comprising 239 people with 200 more hired locally in each city. Each three-hundred-foot-wide stage took twenty-seven hours to assemble and a fleet of fifty-five trucks to transport. The logistics required that one stage would be in use while another was being set up and the third was traveling or broken down, always allowing one crew to rest. Eleven buses carried tour personnel, with the band traveling on planes.

When it was all over McCartney's New World Tour had conquered nineteen countries with a total of seventy-nine shows. For the final show of the American tour and for the first time in his career, McCartney performed a live televised concert at the Blockbuster Pavilion in Charlotte, North Carolina. The show, which aired on Fox Television, resulted in the highest television ratings ever for the channel.

There was no doubt that McCartney's popularity was still strong. Paul opened the brand new Alamodome in San Antonio, Texas, where forty-seven thousand tickets were sold in two hours. At this show a woman stripped from the waist up and offered her bra to the rock star, something that hadn't happened since the days of Beatlemania. After singing "Yesterday," McCartney received a seventy-two-second ovation from the standing audience.

The average ticket price was $32.50, but at some concerts a "Gold Circle" ticket was available starting at $75. These seats lined the front of the stage. For

An amused Paul finds a replica of his vest on a Japanese fan. "Drive My Car," September 14, 1993, Earls Court, London, England.

$1,000 a LIPA (Liverpool Institute for the Performing Arts) charity ticket was offered to the first fifty people at selected venues. Participants were pampered with tickets to the show, VIP parking, an open bar, a gourmet vegetarian dinner, never-before-seen videos for backstage entertainment, a McCartney sound check with cameras allowed, a New World Tour T-shirt, concert program, personalized VIP backstage laminate, and in some cities, a press conference. Proceeds from the LIPA tickets would help support the building fund of McCartney's "Fame School" in Liverpool—a $33 million project launched in 1990 to educate the world's most talented performing-arts students.

There was plenty of merchandise from which to choose: hats, a selection of eight different T-shirts, programs, buttons, sweatshirts, tour jackets, and a backpack. Once again, a free ninety-eight-page program was given to every audience member.

McCartney's band lineup remained the same except for drummer Chris Whitten, who was replaced by Blair Cunningham, a native of Memphis, Tennessee, and alumnus of the Pretenders (Robbie McIntosh's former band), Haircut 100, and Echo & the Bunnymen.

New to this show was an acoustic set, something McCartney had not attempted since his 1975–1976 Wings over the World Tour. The set allowed him to give an "unplugged" feel (sans electric guitars and keyboards) to his music halfway through the concert. McCartney's acclaimed *Unplugged* television show for MTV in 1991 introduced the first song Paul ever wrote (at the age of fourteen), "I Lost My Little Girl," performed to the delight of his European, South American, and Mexican audiences on the New World Tour.

The song list for the American shows included thirty-two songs and one instrumental: "Drive My Car," "Coming Up," "Looking for Changes," "Another Day," "All My Loving," "Let Me Roll It," "Peace in the Neighbourhood," "Off the Ground," "Can't Buy Me Love," "Robbie's Guitar Bit" (instrumental), an acoustic set of "Good Rockin' Tonight," "We Can Work It Out," "And I Love Her," "Every Night," "Hope of Deliverance," "Michelle," "Biker like an Icon," "Here, There, and Everywhere," and "Yesterday." The show continued with "My Love," "Lady Madonna," "Live and Let Die," "Let It Be," "Magical Mystery Tour," "C'mon People," "The Long and Winding Road," "Paperback Writer," "Fixing a Hole," "Penny Lane," "Sgt. Pepper's Lonely Hearts Club Band," and encores "Band on the Run," "I Saw Her Standing There," and "Hey Jude."

In Europe, Mexico, and South America, some songs were substituted, including: "Jet," "I Lost My Little Girl," "Ain't No Sunshine" (with Paul playing drums), and "Back in the USSR." Dropped were: "Get out of My Way" (performed in Australia and New Zealand only), "Another

McCartney, in subdued light, churns out intricate bass runs during the heavy percussion interlude of "Coming Up." September 14, 1993, Earls Court, London, England.

Day," "And I Love Her," "Every Night," "Fixing a Hole," and "Long and Winding Road." The cities of Winnipeg and Toronto (Canada), Auckland (New Zealand), and Parramatta (Australia) were treated to "Mull of Kintyre," complete with a local bagpipe band. "Kansas City" was performed only in Kansas City.

Paul did an abbreviated eighty-five-minute set consisting of seventeen songs at the Hollywood Bowl Earth Day Concert on April 16. Songs unique to this show included "Mother Nature's Son" and "Blackbird." He was the last performer of the evening and was joined onstage by k.d. lang, who sang backup vocals for "Hope of Deliverance," and by a bearded Ringo Starr for the concert's grand finale song, "Hey Jude." For the second time since the Beatles's breakup, Paul's ex–band mate joined him onstage—the first time was at the Forum in Inglewood, California, after a 1976 Wings concert. Ringo shared Paul's microphone, singing the "nah, nah, nahs" to "Hey Jude."

The usual McCartney concert lasted 145 minutes and opened with a new twelve-minute film directed by Kevin Godley (formerly of 10cc). This film showcased a musical history of the rock star, with some never-before-seen footage of the Beatles, interesting home movies of the McCartney family, and some graphic scenes of vivisection, animal mutilation, and torture—a powerful but disturbing message that had adults and children in tears. These unsettling images—much more horrific than images from his previous tour—became a turning point for some concertgoers who became enlightened by the McCartneys ongoing campaign against animal cruelty.

As the numbered countdown to the familiar letters N-O-W appeared on the center screen, McCartney and his band casually walked across the fog covered stage. Before he picked up his famous bass guitar, he strolled the length of the stage, waving and mugging to the crowd.

▲ Paul leads the Earth Day volunteers and audience through the refrain of "Hey Jude." This concert featured "Mother Nature's Son" and "Blackbird." McCartney and his band were one of several acts, including Steve Miller, PM Dawn, 10,000 Maniacs, k.d. lang (who sang "Hope of Deliverance" with Paul), emcee Chevy Chase, Kenny Loggins, and Don Henley. Earth Day Concert, April 16, 1993, Hollywood Bowl, Hollywood, California.

▶ A rare photo of Ringo Starr singing onstage with Paul as they share the microphone during "Hey Jude" at the Earth Day Concert, April 16, 1993, Hollywood Bowl, Hollywood, California. Ringo joined Paul in 1976 at the Forum in Inglewood, California (see pages 18–19). Those were the only two times they appeared together onstage after the Beatles's breakup.

McCartney dressed in a tailored black jacket with white pinstripes, reminiscent of his 1966 Beatles jacket. Beneath the jacket would either be a black-and-white satin alphabet vest, a multicolored gold-brocade vest, a gold-and-red-striped vest, or a black-and-white vest with silhouettes of birds in flight. His shirt was white with troubadour sleeves and sometimes trimmed with a black collar and cuffs. Nonleather tennis shoes and black Levis completed the outfit. Linda wore colorful long jackets and scarves designed by daughter Stella.

Gone were the green patterned lasers and strobe lights used so effectively on his last tours. By 1993 those special effects were considered passé. Instead, banks of colored spots illuminated the performers and at times the audience. Artist Brian Clarke once again used abstract backdrops that stood 210 feet wide by almost 100 feet high painted with grids and organic forms that added vibrant colors to complement the stage lighting. McCartney's sound system generated a staggering one million watts—a far cry from the minuscule three Vox amps used on the Beatles's tour.

The show began with "Drive My Car," prompting a variety of exaggerated, rock star poses from McCartney, who charmed the crowd with his stage antics. Two sixty-foot-high video screens, positioned to each side of the stage, served as a visual aid for those seated toward the back of the stadium. The words "Beep beep, beep beep, YEAH!" flashed on the screens ending the song.

McCartney immediately launched into "Coming Up," unleashing a contagious energy that forced even the most sedentary nonfans to their feet. The band was tighter than on the previous tour, producing a gutsier style, fine-tuned and disciplined from four years of McCartney tutoring. Beatles songs that were never performed live remained faithful to the recorded versions with an extra added punch provided by the seasoned touring band.

"Live and Let Die" was again the showstopper. Equipped with an arsenal of pyrotechnic delights, the new explosives—a more intense variety—required very precise calculations when deployed inside a "domed" stadium. Fireworks rose to the limit of the ceiling before they blossomed into a cascade of flickering embers, falling perilously close to the audience below. Unsuspecting concertgoers were shocked as bombs exploded all around the stage. The surprised looks on people's faces seemed to amuse McCartney, who smiled like an impish child misbehaving. McCartney pantomimed at the song's conclusion, mocking the crowd with gestures taken from his own observations. First he beat on his chest and feigned a heart attack, then he closed his eyes, put his fingers in his ears, and grimaced. The silly gestures continued as he made circles with his hands that approximated the size of the explosions—followed by swimming strokes and driving motions. Then he pointed to an imaginary watch and laid his head on his hands, feigning sleep. Lastly, he pounded the top of his piano and struck a pose with a huge grin, drawing a thunderous applause.

"Let It Be" employed a 39,600-square-foot backdrop—almost equivalent to a city block—that simulated stained-glass church windows. At the song's conclusion Paul stood up, walked to the front of the stage, and whistled for his "magic piano." "Come on boy," he called as if to a dog and out rolled a psychedelic, painted piano with flashing neon lights. As if by magic, it slowly rolled across the front of the stage and stopped when Paul commanded, "AND SIT!"

The next song was "Magical Mystery Tour" followed by "C'mon People." Linda's captivating black-and-white photographs of rock stars were projected on the video screens. Familiar faces of Janis Joplin, Aretha Franklin, Jimi Hendrix, and John Lennon appeared, to cheers of the crowd. Linda's photos were displayed during a number of songs, including "Michelle" where images of young French women were shown with scenic city landmarks. "Biker like an Icon" utilized parts of the Marlon Brando film "Wild One" and stained-glass projections of a religious Madonna icon that magically transformed into a female biker with a helmet.

"Paperback Writer," not performed since 1966, deployed hanging vertical sheets with printed words simulating pages in a book or newspaper. At earlier shows, the sheets were blank and used projections of words and/or cloud patterns. The sheets fell dramatically to the floor at the song's end and were hustled away by roadies.

"Sgt. Pepper's Lonely Hearts Club Band" brought out the psychedelic kaleidoscope swirling patterns, reminiscent of the '60s. Heavy fog was pumped onto the stage as the famous jam began

▲ Paul peeks over the top of his psychedelic piano to tease fans in the front row prior to "Magical Mystery Tour." April 20, 1993, Aggie Memorial Stadium, Las Cruces, New Mexico.

▶ McCartney hams it up for the photographers. Unique to this world tour was a Beatles song as the opener. "Drive My Car," September 14, 1993, Earls Court, London, England.

between Paul and Robbie McIntosh. Armed with his Gibson Les Paul, McCartney delivered blistering guitar solos that rivaled his lead guitarist as they dueled, hammering out riffs—one after another. Their mock battle continued with some playful pushing and shoving until Paul finally gave in, throwing his hands in the air.

After the encore, McCartney came onstage waving the flag of the country or city where he was performing. On the screens were satellite maps of the city taken from three hundred miles up.

During the last song, "Hey Jude," Paul and the band were hoisted above the crowd with the help of a mechanical arm (pivot-boom) holding a seven-foot circular platform. The device was also used earlier in the show during "Let Me Roll It." This time Paul led the audience in a sing-along, high atop the moving platform as the band threw confetti and rose petals over the crowd.

"Let me hear you! C'mon NOW! Oh, yeah! Just the people on the RIGHT sing. *[Audience sings, 'nah, nah, nah . . .']* Now the people on the LEFT. *[Points as the audience sings]* Everybody in the MIDDLE sing. C'mon, you got it! *[Audience sings again]* Now the GERLS! WOMEN ONLY! [Leads them like a conductor] Now the MEN! *[Makes a mock body-builder pose, flexing his arms]* Okay, you're on your own now. *[Departs the platform with the band and returns to the piano]* ONE MORE TIME! Nah, nah, nah . . . Hey-ay, JUDE-A-JU-DAY, JUDE. *[Ends song]* You were GREAT and YOU were great. . . , and YOU were. . . !" *[Points to people in the crowd]*

Before McCartney left the stage for the last time, he returned once more to the microphone and promised, "See ya next time!"

First encore after "Sgt. Pepper's Lonely Hearts Club Band." The second show at Earls Court. September 14, 1993, London, England.

I SAW HIM

November 20, 1993,
Kyushu to Narita,
Japan

I was waiting with my friend in the VIP lounge at Hakata Airport for my flight from Kyushu to Narita (near Tokyo) when Paul and his family walked in. Paul had finished his last concert the evening before at the Fukuoka Dome. I froze and couldn't say anything. He must have seen the shocked look on my face and said, "*Konichiwa!*" (Hello!) as he passed me. A Japanese security guard came over and said not to bother them because this was their "private time." It was hard not to look at them sitting in the same room, but I respected their privacy and patiently waited until we were called to board the plane. I noticed Paul was wearing a black suit with matching trousers and a dark royal blue button-down shirt, sans tie.

My friend and I left the airport lounge ahead of the McCartneys and found our first-class seats—in the same row as Paul and Linda! What LUCK! There was an aisle between us and their security people. The McCartney family was in the next section of seats by the window. Paul had the window seat and was reading a book and sitting next to Linda, who was also reading. Linda wore reading glasses, but Paul didn't. Paul must have noticed us staring at him, because he got up, walked over to me and again said, "*Konichiwa!*" with a big smile on his face. I just couldn't move as he got closer to me and picked up my hand to shake it. He said, "Are you going to Narita, too?" I just answered, "Yes!" not knowing what else to say. Then he went back to his seat.

James and Mary were in the row in front of them and when the plane took off and landed, Linda reached over the back of Mary's seat and held her hand. Paul did the same with James.

They had a light meal consisting of vegetable sandwiches, cut apples, oranges, and cheese on crackers. Paul tried to eat the orange, but had trouble peeling it so Linda did it for him.

Hamish and Blair were there and constantly got up to walk around. Paul and Linda stayed quietly in their seats—except for one time when Paul got up to go to the bathroom. The flight lasted one and one-half hours and

▲ McCartney, looking youthful at age fifty, sways to the beat of the music. "Coming Up," June 2, 1993, Milwaukee County Stadium, Milwaukee, Wisconsin.

▶ In reference to the inclement weather, Paul comments that he has never realized how many songs he's written about rain. "Drive My Car," June 2, 1993, Milwaukee County Stadium, Milwaukee, Wisconsin.

during that time Paul took photos out of the window and Linda took photos of fans in the back section of the plane.

A stewardess came over and offered them some postcards, which Linda took and began writing on, then offered Paul some candies and he said politely, "No thank you."

We arrived at Narita International Airport and as Paul was getting off the plane, fans sitting in the economy section yelled, "See you again. Please DON'T GO!" He gave them the thumbs-up as he pushed his way through the crowded airport followed closely by security. Linda, Mary, and James stayed well behind him as fans futilely tried to get past his security people. They boarded a private bus to take them to another flight and left Japan.

I'll never forget that flight, the sky was so blue and Paul McCartney was sitting right there!

—SUMIYO OMORI

▲ "Peace and understanding . . ." Paul flashes the peace sign at the end of "Coming Up." June 2, 1993, Milwaukee County Stadium, Milwaukee, Wisconsin.

◀ A rowdy crowd inspires McCartney's comedic facial expressions. "Coming Up," June 2, 1993, Milwaukee County Stadium, Milwaukee, Wisconsin.

I SAW HIM

December 3, 1993,
Pacaembu Stadium,
São Paulo, Brazil

A few hours before the show, I decided to try and see the sound check. When the sound check started I was content just to listen, but after a while I decided to walk up the stadium hill (it's a very high place) and find a crack in one of the walls to peer through. My little excursion paid off. I could clearly see Paul onstage, wearing white baggy trousers, a striped T-shirt, black jacket, and sunglasses. For the next two hours, I watched and listened to him sing a mix of tunes that included songs not performed at the actual concert.

He played: "Matchbox," "Just Because," "Crackin' Up," "I Wanna Be Your Man," "Off the Ground," "Midnight Special," "Things We Said Today," "We Can Work It Out," "Good Rockin' Tonight," "Honey Don't," "C Moon," "The Long and Winding Road," "Ain't That a Shame," "Don't Let the Sun Catch You Crying," "Get out of My Way," "Another Day," and "Twenty Flight Rock."

Paul took every opportunity to address our group (three hundred had gathered) and asked us, "*O Som está bom?*" (Is the sound okay?) He asked one of my friends if the sound was too low and my friend told him it was terrific! During "C Moon" instead of the usual Jamaican rap at the end, he threw in some Portuguese phrases like, "*Tudo bem?*" (Is that alright?) and "*Obrigado, São Paulo!*" (Thank you, São Paulo!). That provoked giggles from the crowd. He jumped around with his Hofner bass doing silly gestures, including butt shaking, leaping, and uncoordinated dancing. It was a performance I will never forget.

—CLAUDIO D. DIRANI

Sound check at Anaheim Stadium. Paul looks right into my lens while playing his guitar. He played continuously, even between songs. April 17, 1993, Anaheim, California.

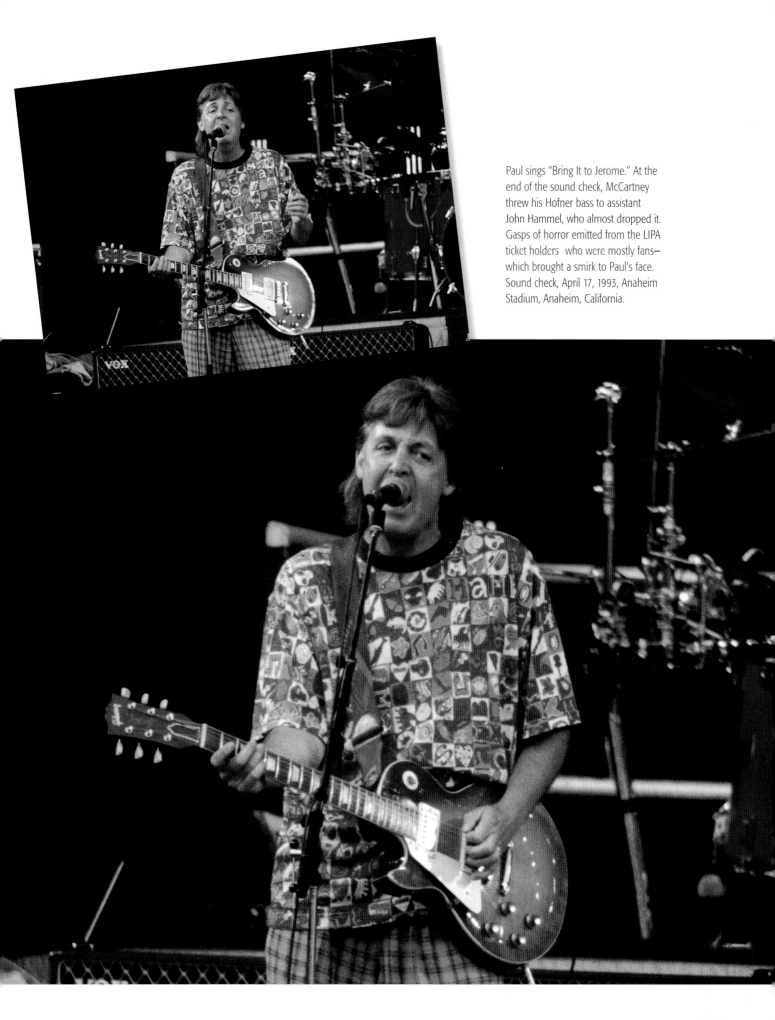

Paul sings "Bring It to Jerome." At the end of the sound check, McCartney threw his Hofner bass to assistant John Hammel, who almost dropped it. Gasps of horror emitted from the LIPA ticket holders who were mostly fans—which brought a smirk to Paul's face. Sound check, April 17, 1993, Anaheim Stadium, Anaheim, California.

▲ "That was for all the lovers in the audience." "My Love," April 20, 1993, Aggie Memorial Stadium, Las Cruces, New Mexico.

▶ A Macca chipmunk face for Robbie as Paul duels guitar solos with him. "Sgt. Pepper's Lonely Hearts Club Band," April 20, 1993, Aggie Memorial Stadium, Las Cruces, New Mexico.

I SAW HIM

September 27 and 28, 1993, Oslo Spektrum, Oslo, Norway

Paul held two concerts in Oslo during the New World Tour and the Norwegian press ran a series of negative articles about Paul's antiwhaling campaign. There were massive attacks on Paul from whalers: "A pop star can't come here and tell us to put away our ancient culture, take away food, and tell us how to live!" The mood became very tense prior to his arrival.

I made a banner that read, "Stop the Whaling! I'd rather be listening to Macca!" I hoped it would draw Paul's and Linda's attention. At the first show it caught Paul's eye and he acknowledged it with a nod and several thumbs-up.

One of the best things about the show was that the media expected antiwhaling statements from the stage and never got it. They even brought in whalers to make a spectacle out of the McCartneys's reactions. Instead, they had to write great reviews about a spectacular rock show!

The next night my banner was immediately recognized by Paul who mouthed a few hellos and gave more thumbs-up. Toward the end of the concert I didn't know what to do with it, so I threw it to Robbie. He picked it up and showed it to Wix. Paul and Linda were at the opposite end of the stage, taking their final bows. Then a curious Linda came over, looked at the banner, laughed, and asked Robbie to hold one of the ends. Paul followed, stared at the banner, and had a brief discussion with Linda. It seemed that Linda had the final decision and she unfolded the banner, showing it to the audience—a very bold move on her part, considering the brewing controversy about their statements. Many booed the banner, but just as many applauded—ironically, no journalist was in sight! In the meantime, Paul concentrated on his throwing ability and tossed out his towel (unfortunately, not in my direction).

Linda appeared to ask where the banner came from and both Robbie and Paul pointed to me. Then she gave me a big smile, with two thumbs-up, and blew a kiss in my direction. I nearly fainted!

Linda left the stage with the banner and I hope it became part of the most interesting collection of fan souvenirs gathered by a rock star. This was the last time I saw her and I will forever cherish that moment.

—HELGE HALKJELSVIK

I SAW HIM

May 5, 1993, Riverfront Stadium, Cincinnati, Ohio

In 1993, during the New World Tour, I was expecting my son and had a terrible bout of morning sickness. I hoped that our fifteenth-row tickets, obtained through the Paul McCartney Fun Club (McCartney's official fan club), would help me forget how sick I was. Paul's music had a healing power of its own and I was sure that *seeing* Paul would definitely be a cure!

During the show I felt much better thanks to Paul. It was an awesome concert with a different repertoire from the previous tour, including my favorite *Off the Ground* material. The music let me forget how bad I was feeling.

To this day, my son loves Paul McCartney and we're sure it's because he heard so much of his music before he was born! In fact, he may have been the "youngest" McCartney fan at that concert!

—DEBBIE CLEGG

◄ A party followed the third show at this venue where Paul met up with his old band mate George Harrison. "Coming Up," September 14, 1993, Earls Court, London, England.

▲ McCartney greets his countrymen at Earls Court in London, England, September 14, 1993. One bold fan yelled out, "Get it right!" during "Yesterday." From that moment on Paul had to restrain himself from laughing. He doubled over with laughter at the end of the song.

I SAW HIM

April 27, 1993, Liberty Bowl Memorial Stadium, Memphis, Tennessee

When Paul played Memphis he goofed up the words to "We Can Work It Out," stopping the band midsong. "Hang on, hang on," he said. "I've only got the words wrong again. . . . It's become part of the act. I did this on *Unplugged!*" He added, "This has only happened once before!"

Afterward, McCartney recalled a 1966 Beatles concert next door at the Mid-South Coliseum when he and John began singing two different songs. Paul commented, "I reckon this is an improvement!"

—CHRIS LESHER

Paul falls to his knees after "I Saw Her Standing There." September 11, 1993, Earls Court, London, England.

I SAW HIM

May 9, 1993, Florida Citrus Bowl, Orlando, Florida

I had gotten a verbal "guarantee" from the concert promoter in Ft. Lauderdale that my name would be at the gate when Paul came to speak to the media. I arrived with a DAT recorder and a pad full of questions to ask. After being turned away at the press gate repeatedly for a half an hour, someone from Capitol Records recognized me and swung the gate open. I raced to a waiting seat in the second row under a portable tent and plugged my machine into the audio feed to record the press conference.

McCartney was introduced by a Blockbuster corporate executive, who said Paul was there to announce his first (in decades) live concert broadcast in the United States (on Fox Television) to be held on June 15, at the Blockbuster Pavilion in Charlotte, North Carolina.

The press started in with their usual milktoast questions: "Why did you choose Orlando to make this announcement?" "Are you nervous performing in front of a live audience of this size?" Paul was a master at answering the most banal questions in an interesting and sometimes humorous manner. Here are some of the questions and Paul's answers.

◄◄ Paul leans against a pole in the press tent, amused that nobody (except for me) recognizes him. April 16, 1993, Earth Day Concert, Hollywood Bowl, Hollywood, California.

◄ McCartney answers a question about the environment when a man yells out, "PAUL, I LOVE YOU!" He quickly answers, "Hey, love you, too. [Laughs] I don't even *know you* and *I love you!*" April 16, 1993, Earth Day Concert, Hollywood Bowl, Hollywood, California.

Paul: Hi there. How y'doing? Hello! *[Big applause]* Thank you for that very warm reception. Don't stop! Don't stop! No, no, no. Thank you! Thank you very much. Lady in the front. Hi lady.

Q: This is the first time in your career that you've done a concert televised live. Why are you doing this now?

Paul: Someone asked me to do it. I said, "Yeah, that sounds like a good idea. . . . The band likes to play." We like to show off. So, we figured it's a challenge . . . 'bout time we do it.

Q: Why did you decide to do it on free network TV instead of pay-per-view?

Paul: Good question. I've no idea. They asked me to do it and I just said, "Yeah, it sounds like a good idea. I'll do it."

Q: What can viewers expect from the show?

Rhythmic, flashing blue lights, a photographer's nightmare, capture an unpretentious Paul. "Coming Up," June 2, 1993, Milwaukee County Stadium, Milwaukee, Wisconsin.

Paul: We're trying to give them the best little show in town. We hope that they'll take home some great memories. They might even remember it the rest of their lives. We're trying to give 'em some good music. We're trying to play well and there's a little bit of a message attached, which is to do with helping out this old planet of ours. So, basically, that's what we're trying to bring 'em.

"Penny Lane," September 15, 1993, Earls Court, London, England.

Q: Will this show be available later on tape?

Paul: I'm not sure of the situation. I think at the moment it's not planned to be available on tape, but you never know. If it can work out, great. It might do. *[Joe Johnson says, "I'll tape it for you!"]* Yeah. *[Giggles]* He'll tape it for ya! *[Reporters laugh]*

Q: Is this potentially the largest audience that you and your band will have ever played to? Does that intimidate you at all? Are you excited?

Paul: Umm . . . Will it be as large as the *Ed Sullivan Show*? *[Reporters howl with laughter]* GOTCHA! Gotcha!

But, yeah, I mean, sure, it'll intimidate me, sure. But that's showbiz, you know. But no, I'm looking forward to it. It's . . . aah . . . going to be quite fun, I think?

Q: Is there some special guest on the show?

Paul: At the moment we're really going to just do our show as it stands. You know, we may do a few little special things. But it's basically to bring the show to your living room. . . . We've played to a lot of people. We've played to like thirty or forty thousand each night, but inevitably there's a few people who'll miss it. So from my point of view it's to try and reach those people in their living rooms when they least suspect it.

Paul charms the soaked Milwaukee audience. Concertgoers spent hours tailgating outside the stadium before the doors opened. After Paul arrived, around 5:00 P.M., the rain started and continued throughout the night. "Coming Up," June 2, 1993, Milwaukee County Stadium, Milwaukee, Wisconsin.

McCartney hammers away on his famous Hofner bass. "Drive My Car," June 2, 1993, Milwaukee County Stadium, Milwaukee, Wisconsin.

Q: Why did you choose Orlando for this press conference?

Paul: Ah, it chose *me,* actually. Some man came up to me and said, "We're doing a press conference in Orlando." *[Reporters laugh]* I said, "It sounds okay by me, gov!" That's why we're doing it here.

Joe Johnson: A lot of us have great memories of the Beatles days—and Wings even. And a lot of us have collectible items: dolls, wigs, and things. What is your most prized possession that you have from those days?

Paul: Probably my Hofner bass. Which is, you know . . . *[Someone claps]* Ha! Thank you! My Hofner bass thanks you. *[Reporters laugh]* I'll tell her later. It was an instrument I got back in the '60s and it still has the old gig list stuck to the side, you know, from one of the old . . . I think from the last Beatles show. So, it's a cheap little instrument, but you know, it's my favorite. It's probably a great sort of souvenir from those times and it sounds good, too!

▲ "Paperback Writer," April 20, 1993, Aggie Memorial Stadium, Las Cruces, New Mexico. The explosions were so loud at this show that when Paul finished "Live and Let Die," he said, "That one woke the neighbors up. Yee! HA . . . ! The guy who does the bangs is called Shaky. . . ."

▶ Paul takes the opportunity to make faces at someone in the front row as he bends down to pick up some flowers. April 20, 1993, Aggie Memorial Stadium, Las Cruces, New Mexico.

Q: Two-part question. What are you going to play for President Clinton when you perform at the White House? And you've been doing press conferences for thirty years, what question haven't you been asked that you'd like to answer?

Paul: Well, I've been asked that one! *[People laugh and clap]* What are we going to do for President Clinton? I'm not really sure yet. I think we're playing in quite a small room in the White House . . . if it happens. You never know with these things. . . . If there's some big sort of news event that happens, obviously his attention has got to be distracted. I'd be the first to say, "Listen, you go deal with the crisis. We won't play." But, I mean if we do play, and it would be nice to do it . . . *[Reporter yells, "Are you going to let him sit in?"]* Pardon? *[Reporter repeats the question]* Yeah, just in the front. *[People laugh]*

　　If he wants to play, I don't know, you know. YEAH, SURE! *[Giggles]* If he wants to play, I'm not going to say, "NO!" *[Press laughs]* Sure, it'd be GREAT actually.

　　Well I think we'd pretty much do sort of an acoustic set, 'cause it's a small place. We can't really get all the big show in there. It should be good fun.

Q: Paul, any particular reason you've decided not to play your Rickenbacker in the past couple of tours?

Paul: No real definite reason. I got a few basses that I could play. I've just got back into playing my Hofner. When I was working with Elvis Costello, he requested that I kind of get it out of mothballs. I haven't been playing it for quite a while 'cause it's . . . The tuning is not very reliable right up at the top of the neck. But I don't often go there anyway. And we worked on it. The tuning's a bit better now. So, I just got back into using the Hofner. It's very light to play. I love the "Ricky," but the Hofner's real nice, too, you know. So, I'm just using that, this tour.

Sweat sprays from McCartney's towel, which was thrown to some lucky fan at the end of the show. He says, "They must have been able to hear us from fifty miles around, I reckon." April 20, 1993, Aggie Memorial Stadium, Las Cruces, New Mexico.

Q: **You're stressing a lot of environmental and animal rights concerns on this tour. Realistically, what kind of impact do you think you can make with music as far as that goes?**

Paul: Well, you know, I mean that's a good question. If people say, "Well . . . celebrities . . . can they make any effect on the real issues?" The way I look at it is, in many ways, we're the voice of the people I meet. The people I meet will talk about this and be very interested, obviously, in saving the planet—many of them in protecting animal rights. But no one is going to listen to them. They can't command these press conferences. So, rather than just use these to talk about me, a record, or the gigs, I do like to try and introduce other issues that are important to me—so people know how you're thinking. Yeah, I think it's good for people to have an update as to what you think and . . . realistically, I think you can have some very interesting effects.

Sometimes I would cite John [Lennon]'s writing—"Give Peace a Chance," for instance—at the end of the Vietnam War. When you see the film of what is near a million people, singing that song to Nixon at the White House, I'm sure it has some effect. . . . He's sitting in there listening to all those people sing "Give Peace a Chance." Those are his voters. So, I think whilst environmental things can't just be cleaned up instantly, 'cause they are expensive, I'd like to try and direct people's thinking and focus it toward that. If they think I'm just doing it for my own career, well I say, "Look, you sort it out. You get the governments to sort it out and I'll sit down. You clean up these oil spills. You close that hole in the sky. I promise I won't say anymore. But till then . . . I'm a father of four kids, you know. I want to see this place get sorted."

Publicist: **Ladies and gentlemen I'm afraid we have to go and do a show.**

Paul: We're gonna do a show? *[Looks surprised]* Okay, folks! That appears to be it! Thank you very much. Thank you. *[Applause, Paul exits quickly]*

At the end of the conference, a rather short one, Paul became an autograph Houdini. By now he knew the routine and made his exit stage right, before any members of the press could rush him for a signature.

—JOE JOHNSON (of the syndicated radio show *Beatle Brunch*)

▶ McCartney savagely attacks the vocals on "Sgt. Pepper's Lonely Hearts Club Band," surrounded by a psychedelic backdrop of kaleidoscope rotating projections. Earls Court, September 15, 1993, London, England.

▶▶ A silhouetted Paul gives the London audience a guitar salute after "Sgt. Pepper's Lonely Hearts Club Band." September 15, 1993, Earls Court, London, England.

November 25 and 27, 1993, Autódromo Hermanos Rodriguez, Mexico City, Mexico

Outside the Autódromo cars lined every street as they slowly made their way to the parking lots. People were everywhere and close to seventy souvenir dealers were doing a brisk business of selling memorabilia, including T-shirts, lighters, bootlegs, two different Coca-Cola cans with Paul's face on them, license-plate holders, photos, jackets, buttons, vests, underwear, and clocks.

When I entered the stadium, I was handed a free program encased in a special plastic liner from Coca-Cola, the tour sponsor. Near the stage, guards carried automatic weapons and other security personnel held long wooden clubs. During the show they would not allow people to dance on the chairs or move from their seats.

At 8:20 P.M. the lights turned off and the movie began. As scenes of animals being tortured appeared on screen, my life changed forever. For many years I had been a meat eater, but from that moment on I became a vegetarian.

Paul appeared onstage smiling and waving to the audience of 52,122 who took a few seconds to react to his presence. We were in shock to see a live Beatle right in front of us!

Following "Coming Up" Paul spoke in Spanish and said, "*Hola, Mexico!*" (Hello, Mexico!) The audience reaction was instantaneous with screams of approval. He added, "*Hablo poco español, estamos contentos de estar en México.*" (I speak a little Spanish and we are happy to be in Mexico.)

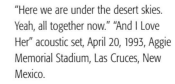

"Here we are under the desert skies. Yeah, all together now." "And I Love Her" acoustic set, April 20, 1993, Aggie Memorial Stadium, Las Cruces, New Mexico.

Throughout the show people would flash cigarette lighters on and off. Paul seemed pleased with this display and said, "*Muchas gracias!*" (Thank you very much!)

We almost understood everything Paul said in English and there was good communication between him and the audience. People clapped and sang along to his songs, with the newer music from *Off the Ground* receiving as much enthusiasm as the Beatles's songs.

He introduced "I Lost My Little Girl" in Spanish saying, "*Esta es la primera canción que escribí cuando tenía catorce años.*" (This is the first song I ever wrote when I was fourteen years old.) Many of us in the audience knew the words and he seemed very impressed and said again, "*Muchas gracias!*"

At the end of "Can't Buy Me Love" the crowd sang a special *porra* (rhythmic chant) to Paul: "Chiquit bum a la bim, bom, baaa! Paul, Paul, rah, rah, rah!" The band joined in and Paul replied, "*Viva Mexico!*" (Long live Mexico!) I'm going to play the drums now, YEAH, *SÍ, SÍ, SÍ!*" He took over the drums while Hamish Stuart sang and played guitar on "Ain't No Sunshine."

The last song of the show was "Hey Jude" and for the chorus he requested, "*Solo hombres!* (Men only!) And now, *Solo mujeres!*" (Women only!) For the final bows the band came out wearing mariachi hats called *sombreros de charro* (large-brimmed Mexican hats).

After the show Paul, Linda, and James left the Autódromo in a special bus for the airport. A limousine was used as a decoy for waiting fans who ran after it screaming, never knowing that the McCartneys were safely on their way to Acapulco.

On the twenty-seventh, the McCartneys returned for the final show and some highlights included the band's rendition of a traditional song from Guadalajara called, "El Jarabe Tapatio." They sang a fragment of it just before "Hey Jude" and the audience responded with "*VIVA! VIVA!*" Paul shouted back "*VIVA MEXICO!* Okay! Alright! *Muchas gracias!* Really! We've had a great time in Mexico City. Thank you very much! *Hasta la vista!*" (See you soon!) Before he left, a fan handed Paul a Spanish guitar, which he signed and gave back to him.

Both shows were great and I have to thank Paul and Linda because they changed my life. Now I'm veggie, my health is better, and I'm very happy!

—CLAUDIA LETICIA ESPINOSA

◀ McCartney comes onstage after the first encore waving the New Mexico state flag. April 20, 1993, Aggie Memorial Stadium, Las Cruces, New Mexico.

▶ Paul tries out his Spanish. *"Muchos gracias, Las Cruces! Tres conejos, en un árbol . . .* (Thank you very much, Las Cruces! Three rabbits in a tree . . .) *[Laughs]* Don't ask!" "Every Night" acoustic set, April 20, 1993, Aggie Memorial Stadium, Las Cruces, New Mexico.

▲ McCartney kneels signaling the
band with three fingers after "I Saw
Her Standing There." September 15,
1993, Earls Court, London, England.

▶ Paul leans against Robbie as they
trade lead guitar licks during "Sgt.
Pepper's Lonely Hearts Club Band."
September 15, 1993, Earls Court,
London, England.

I SAW HIM

September 11, 1993,
Earls Court, London,
England

I took my wife, JaneP, and three other women to London in 1993—it's a tough job, but somebody's got to do it—because, as usual, she had gotten tickets to *all three* concerts. The seats we had were decent, but nothing great. I was hoping that we could upgrade and get closer to Paul. Once you've seen Paul from the front row, you never want to be any other place!

Tons of ticket touts (scalpers) were hanging around outside Earls Court, but nothing they had was close enough for us. It was getting late and we still had no luck finding better seats.

All of a sudden, I heard JaneP hollering my name. I knew something was up! I've heard that tone in her voice before! A new scalper had come up and she had found *six front-row-center seats!* One for each of us and a spare for a friend.

We brought a big red sign made by a friend that read "I love Paul" on the front and "I love Linda" on the back. (She knew I was a big Linda fan.) During the concert, JaneP and I got Paul's and Linda's attention several times with the signs. Linda got all giddy about it because she wasn't used to men in the audience holding up signs for her! It must have been funny for them to see JaneP and me pretending to fight over the sign—arguing which side we'd show them!

At the end of the show, several people passed flowers up to Paul via the security guards. My "three girlfriends" had made sure that I had a single pink rose for Linda. As I held up the "I love Linda" sign with the rose, Paul saw it, walked across the stage and said to me, "Can I get that for Linda?" I handed it right to him and he turned to hand it to Linda. She looked directly at me with a great big grin and shrugged her shoulders. JaneP snapped a great picture that captured the moment.

The next year JaneP asked Linda to autograph the photo for me while attending a press conference for Linda's line of frozen foods in Chicago. Years later we were lucky enough to talk to Paul at a record signing in London. I told Paul that I was the one who held up the "I love Linda" sign at the concerts. He replied, "It *is* you, isn't it? A Linder fan, are ya? Well, I'll have to say you have great taste in women!"

—JIMMY RUCKER

I SAW HIM

May 29, 1993,
Alamodome, San
Antonio, Texas

Paul was the first act to open the newly built Alamodome. Before he performed "Good Rockin' Tonight" at the beginning of the acoustic set, it was discovered that Hamish Stuart's bass guitar had lost its connection. Paul said, "We were going to do a song there, but we've just lost the bass for a minute. So I'm gonna stop. . . . Okay, I'll tell you what. Would you like to hear a song without bass?" Of course we wanted to hear the song, so Paul improvised. He played his guitar and *sang* the bass part when he wasn't singing the lyrics!

Later, when the problem was finally fixed, Paul said, "We've got bass now! I don't think we need it. . . ." And then he kidded, "I think we're better off *without* the bass player!"

—SUSAN CUSENBARY

▲ Paul spots an enthusiastic fan in the front row. Touts (scalpers) were getting anywhere from $75 to $200 more than the face value of the tickets. "Coming Up," September 14, 1993, Earls Court, London, England.

▶ "Another Day," May 31, 1993, Arrowhead Stadium, Kansas City, Missouri.

"Thank you Missourians and Kansas-sians. We're gonna have a good time tonight! Here we are. We're in Kansas City! It's the summer, open sky, we're gonna let our hair down! Okay? Is everyone having a good time tonight? That song was from the 1970s. This one goes back a little bit further." Intro to "All My Loving," May 31, 1993, Arrowhead Stadium, Kansas City, Missouri.

I SAW HIM

November 25, 1993,
Autódromo Hermanos
Rodriguez, Mexico City,
Mexico

Paul held two concerts in Mexico City scheduled over the Thanksgiving weekend. My husband, Larry, obtained tickets for both concerts and even managed to get a pass for the press conference before the first show. We went to EMI in Mexico City to pick up the tickets and passes. Things got a bit tense, because they had only issued one press pass and would not issue another. We felt ecstatic to be seeing both concerts, but worried about which one of us would attend the press conference—a real test of marriage.

That evening we left early to go to the designated meeting area for the press—the site of the 1990 Olympic games. Larry had brought along a tape recorder and microphone from the radio station where he works so he could call in reports for the morning show.

There were journalists from all over the world waiting to board buses and cars that would take them to the Autódromo. Once there we walked past backstage security and I was able to get through without a press pass hanging around my neck! Larry referred to me as "*EL PRODUCER, EL PRODUCER!*" and that, along with the microphone tucked firmly in my hands, got me through.

From there the photojournalists were taken to one area and everyone else was sent upstairs to a small room outfitted with posters and stand-ups of *Paul Is Live.* (Many found their way into our suitcases.) I sat in the front row on the aisle, figuring Paul had to walk past me on his way to the press table.

◀ As the last notes ring out from "Paperback Writer," Paul points to the cheering audience. Above him are hanging sheets with projections of words, simulating pages in a book. The sheets fell to the stage floor at the song's end, where they were quickly gathered by scurrying roadies. April 20, 1993, Aggie Memorial Stadium, Las Cruces, New Mexico.

▲ Paul has a small technical problem with his piano before "Hey Jude" and finds himself in the dark. "Okay, I'm back on the mike here. I'm back over here. Mr. Spotlight, yeah, this is me. This is ME HERE! Hello, HEL-LOW! He's new to the job. Okay, we've got a little hitch over here. It's just the piano that comes up and guess what? It's got STUCK! [Roadies spring into action] This lightning team of astronauts will sort it out like that! You watch. Now I'm going over here whether it's fixed or not. Yeah, that's near enough isn't it? [Begins to sing] Hey Jude . . ." He then leads the audience in a sing-along from the elevated moving platform. April 20, 1993, Aggie Memorial Stadium, Las Cruces, New Mexico.

Larry and I acted quite professional, setting up our equipment, with hearts racing! No one questioned us and soon the conference began. Paul entered from a door near the front, so my aisle seat strategy had failed. He was dressed in jeans, a white T-shirt, and black blazer. His hair was the perfect length, just below the shoulders, and he seemed very relaxed. Paul greeted the press with "*Buenas tardes.* (Good afternoon.) HELLO! *Buenas noches.* (Good evening.) MEXICO!" Then he took questions from the group. Noise from the preconcert announcer was so loud that after three attempts to hear questions, Paul asked for the windows to be closed.

Larry was the second person to be called on and he asked about the newly released *Paul Is Live* album.

Larry: Tell us about why you decided to do the album cover?

Paul: Ahem . . . *[Clears throat]* Well, I was on tour in America and we were putting out a live album. So I was trying to think of an interesting title for it and you know normally it's kind of "Rockin' across the States" or "Rockin' 'round the World" and stuff. . . . I was looking for something involving the word *live.* . . . Someone had just sent me a film script . . . based on the old rumor "Paul is dead" . . . when I was supposed to be walking across the Abbey Road crossing with the guys. . . . 'Cause I didn't have shoes on, an American deejay said I was *dead* and so it was a crazy thing. It was a publicity thing that happened then, so I just thought "Okay, 'Paul is dead,' we'll call the album 'Paul is live.'" . . . I went back to the crossing and this time I've got *shoes on [Audience laughter]* to prove *I'm alive!*

Larry: What is the dog's name?

Paul: The dog is my son's dog and she's called Arrow.

Kathi: Looks like Martha.

Paul: She looks like Martha, yeah. It's a long tradition in our family. . . . *[Takes a deep breath]*
There's absolutely no reason why I've got a dog there. Actually, I'll tell you the only reason is when I rang up the photographer . . . who did the first cover (*Abbey Road*), Ian McMillan, we happened to start talking about dogs. And he's really keen on dogs. So I said I could bring my dog, and he said that would be great. So, it's really just because the photographer loved dogs.

Q: Music from all over the world is being influenced by modern American pop music. What do you think of that?

Paul: The trouble with popular music is that good American music tends to take over the world. So you find kids in Japan wanting to be American, you find kids in India wanting to be American, and, of course, they each have their own very interesting types of music. You know, here in Mexico . . . there's a lot of roots music. A lot of music I love comes from Mexico, because I love guitars; I love guitar-based music. I had a couple of guitars made here in Guadalajara. *[Reporters applaud]* I love the music. I love mariachi and that kind of stuff. . . . I learned a bit of Spanish in school, so . . . I am kind of interested in the whole thing.

A moody shot of Paul caught in a feathered spotlight. "Coming Up," June 2, 1993, Milwaukee County Stadium, Milwaukee, Wisconsin.

Then the publicist announced "one last question" and soon Paul stood, raised his water glass to the audience, and said his farewells: "Thank you! *Adiós! Gracias!*" He quickly left through the same door from which he had entered. Realizing this to be my last moment, I jumped up and yelled, "PAUL!" He had already left the room and seemed a bit startled to hear his name and stepped back in, whereupon I stretched out my hand and shook his! What a wonderful feeling to have finally connected with PAUL!

After he left I sat in his chair and held the microphone he used while Larry took my photo. The smile on my face told the story better than words can convey. My scrapbook repeatedly shows the phrase "dreams do come true" and that is truly how I felt.

After meeting and touching Paul, I gained more confidence in realizing other goals. If you have a strong enough desire, you can make things happen. This meeting is one of my fondest memories and I'll never grow tired of relating it to others! As fate would have it, my dream came true on Thanksgiving Day!

Mexico City was the last McCartney concert we attended, but we hold fast to the dream that more Macca encounters are on the horizon for us. After all, dreams *do* come true!

—KATHI GOODMAN

My husband and I were lucky enough to see Paul from front-row-center seats. Knowing how close we were, I brought my binoculars anyway.

During an opportune moment, I zeroed in on his left hand as he was playing the guitar and examined his wedding ring. When I finished looking, I lowered the binoculars to find that Paul was staring at me with an odd but amused expression on his face. He shook an index finger at me as if he were scolding, then mouthed the words "naugh-ty, naugh-ty!"

That's when I realized, from his perspective, it looked like I was staring at an *entirely* different part of his anatomy. Yikes! I was mortified, but he just tossed his head back and laughed. I suppose if he *really* thought I was staring at his, um, you know what, he sure didn't seem to mind. On the other hand, I prefer to think he actually knew I was looking at his hand and was just kidding.

I'll never know for sure, but either way it was definitely an embarrassing Macca moment to remember.

—DJ

◄ Paul and Hamish bop to the beat of "Drive My Car," June 2, 1993, Milwaukee County Stadium, Milwaukee, Wisconsin.

▲ "Coming Up," Earls Court, London, England, September 14, 1993. This song featured some very silly dancing by Paul that included uncoordinated hand and leg movements and butt waving.

I SAW HIM

April 22, 1993, Astrodome, Houston, Texas

I wanted really great seats for Paul's show and ordered tickets through the Official Paul McCartney Fun Club. I was not disappointed—my seats were in the VIP section, ten rows from the stage. There were celebrities like Carl Lewis and others who my husband attempted to point out to me. All I saw was Paul's Hofner bass guitar onstage, very close to me! Suddenly I became very lightheaded and began to hyperventilate. The excitement was getting to me and Paul had yet to take the stage!

Attempting to breathe slowly and normally again, I busied myself with my concert bag. Inside was the microcassette recorder I brought to tape the concert, a camera that was promptly confiscated by a guard (and returned later), two lighters for the candle tribute, and binoculars, which I didn't need, but would give me a closer look at Paul. I was still breathing in and out slowly. Thank God for time to compose myself before the concert started.

The movie came on and the word N-O-W appeared. Then the screen lifted and out walked Paul himself, launching into "Drive My Car." WOW! I just could not take my eyes off of him.

During the third song my husband pointed out several people from our area walking to the stage. He was too much of a gentleman to push his way there, but he encouraged me to go. As if I needed any real encouragement! Somehow, my body seemed to float to the stage and landed in the spot *right in front of Paul!*

As the song ended Paul shouted a "thank you" to the audience and looked down where I was standing. He smiled, tilted his head, and sort of squinted one eye with a silly little expression on his face. I had no idea what he was doing and never dreamed he was even noticing me until I heard some people near me say: "Who is she? Maybe he knows her. . . . He's pretending to look down her V-necked sweater!" I looked up and met Paul's eyes. He smiled a wicked smile, raised

▶ A lucky fan gets the "eye" from Macca. "Drive My Car," June 2, 1993, Milwaukee County Stadium, Milwaukee, Wisconsin.

▶▶ Paul assumes the "rock star" pose during the concert opener, "Drive My Car." The show at Milwaukee County Stadium was nearly canceled because the sound system went out during a torrential rain that continued for most of the concert. Sound was restored at the last minute. Paul commented, "You know, that's the nicest collection of raincoats I've seen all year." June 2, 1993.

"Yesterday," the emotional highlight of the show. September 15, 1993, Earls Court, London, England.

his eyebrow, and *did it again!* Seizing the moment, my modest self told me that "this is Paul and what the heck!" With a grin, I looked him in the eyes and gave my sweater a slight downward tug (revealing very little actually). This brought a big smile to his face and before starting the next song, he pointed to me, and mouthed, "You're *bad!*"

Throughout the concert he occasionally teased and made quick silly faces at me. I could not believe how charming he was and felt grateful to be this close! With the heat of the stage lights and the thrill of it all, I became light-headed again. I stopped moving to the music and mentally slapped myself, hoping to clear my head—no passing out and missing this! Paul apparently noticed and waved his finger, motioning me to sing along. When I did, he nodded and smiled.

During "Sgt. Pepper's Lonely Hearts Club Band" I was swaying to the music. When Paul sang "you're such a lovely audience" he gave me a cute, raised-eyebrow look. With "we'd love to take you home . . ." he pointed toward me. I responded by casually holding my hands out as if to say "okay!" He shook his head with a smile and continued the song. I smiled at Linda who gave me a little grimace before returning my smile.

Toward the end of the concert Paul, Linda, Robbie, Wix, and Blair went up over the crowd on a hydraulic lift. Linda was throwing confetti with rose petals to the crowd below and, as they came overhead, she looked down and pointed to me. Then she dumped the remainder of her confetti on top of me and grinned. All in good fun, of course!

I felt sad knowing the concert was almost over and wishing it would never end. When the final note played, just before Paul joined Linda and the band for bows, I received one last thrill. Paul held out his guitar pick to me and said, "Want this?" He smiled and motioned that I'd have to catch it. "Ready?" he asked. "YES!" I replied as it fell near a security guard who picked it up and tried to hand it to me as it was snatched by a man who dove forward, disappearing into the crowd with my prize! I looked up at Paul who shrugged and said, "Sorry luv," pulling both pants pockets out to show me he had no more.

After all the bows were taken, they left the stage and I stood there waiting for my husband. When he arrived I cried, "I didn't catch the guitar pick and I could have handed Paul and Linda flowers or a gift!" Suddenly I had this unreal feeling like it had all been a dream. My husband, who had seen it all, said, "Wow! He actually talked to *you!*" Then I reached into my pocket and breathed a sigh of relief as I felt the handful of confetti. It wasn't a dream.

—CATHY CARPENTER

▲ The pick used by Paul during the Anaheim concert, April 17, 1993, Anaheim Stadium, Anaheim, California.

◄ Paul acknowledges the applause at the end of the show. This was the only concert at which Paul performed "Kansas City." May 31, 1993, Arrowhead Stadium, Kansas City, Missouri.

The band moves on a platform high over the audience during a sing-along of "Hey Jude." Linda tosses out confetti and rose petals from an ornate bag, which was attached to the pole in front of her. Due to rain the platform stayed close to the canopy of the stage, keeping the band dry. June 2, 1993, Milwaukee County Stadium, Milwaukee, Wisconsin.

I SAW HIM

March 13, 1993, The Oval, Adelaide, Australia

I have a beautiful memory attached to the Adelaide concert: I personally wished Paul and Linda a happy twenty-fourth wedding anniversary. Some friends and I waited for Paul to arrive at the sound check, but found out he missed it due to a delay in his plane's arrival. We were disappointed and walked back toward the hotel, stopping at an intersection where we waited for the light to change. As I whacked the "walk" button two stretch limos pulled up and stopped at the lights—not more than three feet in front of us. I leaned forward to look into the dark windows when Paul opened them. Within licking distance of my tongue, Paul executed a perfect "thumbs aloft" and said, "How ya doin' . . . ?" He stretched out his hand for me to shake and I leaned forward so Linda could see me. "Hey, happy anniversary guys!" I said with amazing calm. "Wow! Thanks!" replied Paul. With that I relinquished his hand so my friends could have a chance to shake it and say hello.

All too soon the lights turned green and the limo literally sailed off into the sunset, but not before another perfect "thumbs aloft" from Macca. We stood there totally dumbstruck at what had just transpired.

Later at the show, I held up my sign that read "Happy Anniversary, Macca and Gertrude." Upon seeing it, Paul and Linda showered me with airborne kisses and waves.

—GREG SWAN

Paul and Linda take their bows and gifts from fans after "Sgt. Pepper's Lonely Hearts Club Band." Following was a brief intermission and the show resumed with "Band on the Run." September 11, 1993, Earls Court, London, England.

▲ "Yesterday," September 11, 1993, Earls Court, London, England.

◀ A triumphant Paul raises his Les Paul guitar high overhead and salutes the audience after a roaring ovation. "Sgt. Pepper's Lonely Hearts Club Band," September 11, 1993, Earls Court, London, England.

I SAW HIM

March 27, 1993, Western Springs Stadium, Auckland, New Zealand

I was incredibly excited as I entered the gates of Western Springs Stadium. I jostled for position with 50,000 others who had the same purpose—to see PAUL McCARTNEY! Paul didn't disappoint us—wearing black Levis, a white shirt, and an alphabet vest, he unveiled a new set of Beatles songs, some reworked for the acoustic format.

"Drive My Car" opened the show, followed by "Coming Up." The fifth number was "All My Loving," a song that Paul last played with the Beatles in New Zealand almost thirty years earlier.

Guns and Roses had just released their version of "Live and Let Die," but that night Paul put on a performance to rival the American heavy-metal band, complete with lasers and pyrotechnic explosions. He introduced it by saying, "The next song we're gonna do was recently covered by another group!"

McCartney took us one stop further on his magical mystery tour, pulling out his acoustic guitar for "Mull of Kintyre." It was magic—and that was before he brought on the local New Zealand Continental Airlines Pipe Band to accompany him. There is something about the drone of bagpipes that just sends shivers down my spine; and to see it performed live was just incredible.

That night was Wix's birthday, so we joined Paul and the band in singing "Happy Birthday." It was also a special day for the New Zealand cricket team, who defeated the English side. Paul congratulated the team.

The final song was, what else, "Hey Jude." And for perhaps five minutes after Paul had vacated the stage, the air was filled with the sound of fifty thousand people singing the song's refrain.

Thanks, Paul, for taking an often sad world and making it better with your songs.

—MALCOLM ATKINSON

▶ Paul notices a familiar face in the photo pit. "Coming Up," September 14, 1993, Earls Court, London, England.

▶▶ McCartney flashes the peace sign during "Coming Up." September 15, 1993, Earls Court, London, England.

▲ Paul waves to fans waiting outside the hotel following Linda's "food" press conference. Linda snaps a photo as the car drives by. Seconds later McCartney stops the limo in the middle of a street for a fan and allows the rest of her friends to get autographs. May 10, 1994, Chicago, Illinois.

▶ The McCartneys came to Chicago to launch Linda's line of frozen vegetarian dinners. A press conference and tasting was set up promptly at noon, but Paul and Linda were a half-hour late because they were watching a solar eclipse. Paul points to Linda, who gives me a smile at the photo opportunity following the press conference. May 10, 1994, Chicago, Illinois.

◀ Linda waves from the elevator, which just happened to open on my floor of the hotel. As friends scrambled to get their Linda McCartney cookbooks for autographs—knocking a very surprised hotel porter over in the melee—Linda posed for my camera. In the far left-hand corner is daughter Mary McCartney. With Linda are security and personal assistants. May 10, 1994, Linda's Frozen Vegetarian Dinners press launch, Chicago.

▼ More posing from the famous couple. After the photo op, the press turned into fans and showered Paul with albums and photos to sign. He reluctantly signed as many as he could and took an envelope of photos from me and asked, "A prezzie for ME?" May 10, 1994, Linda's Frozen Vegetarian Dinners press launch, Chicago, Illinois.

▲ A young Beatles fan travels all the way from Germany to meet Paul and gets her *Flaming Pie* album signed. October 16, 1997, HMV record signing, London, England.

▶ Paul meets "Nipper," the HMV mascot, and is presented with the Composer of the Century Award by the music store. October 16, 1997, HMV record signing, London, England.

▲ HMV Music Store on Oxford Street welcomes Paul at a record signing. More than ten thousand fans lined both sides of the street, bringing London's busiest shopping district to a standstill. McCartney opened the newly renovated store as a return favor. Back in 1963 Brian Epstein gave producer George Martin an early Beatles demo tape. The fateful meeting was arranged by HMV and led to the Beatles first contract. This was Paul's first U.K. record signing in thirty years. October 16, 1997, HMV record signing, London, England.

◄ McCartney grabs the attention of the HMV crowd to let them know that it's time for him to go. Before he leaves he says goodbye to everyone and says, "Thank you, Jorie, for the photos!" He also pretends to "steal" some CDs on the way out of the music store. October 16, 1997, HMV record signing, London, England.

▲ Morning rehearsals for Paul who arrives at Carnegie Hall to listen to his classical work performed by the Orchestra of St. Luke's and the New York Choral Artists. American Lawrence Foster was the conductor for both the U.K. and U.S. premieres. Celebs in attendance for the performance were Paul Simon, Alec Baldwin, and Elvis Costello. "Standing Stone" premiere, November 19, 1997, New York, New York.

▶ The famous McCartney thumbs-up! He signals waiting fans that he will be stopping the car to chat. May 2, 1997, Abbey Road Studios, London, England. "Standing Stone" recording sessions.

McCartney stands in front of the London Symphony Orchestra (LSO) truck, parked in the Abbey Road Studios parking lot. The symphony was recording Paul's second classical piece, "Standing Stone." The album charted at number one on the American charts and stayed there for eleven weeks. May 2, 1997, London, England. "Standing Stone" recording sessions.

▶ Paul takes *my* picture outside the Carnegie Hall stage door. He was greeted by hundreds of fans, who braved the freezing cold to catch a glimpse of their idol who was in town for the U.S. premiere of his classical work "Standing Stone." November 19, 1997, New York, New York.

▶ Photo call at the Royal Albert Hall, London, England. Paul stands like Superman while flashes pop from seventy-five world press photographers. He was there rehearsing for the premiere of "Standing Stone," which was performed by the London Symphony Orchestra. October 14, 1997.

▼ Onstage with the London Symphony Orchestra, Paul acknowledges the standing ovation from the full house of 4,800. Paul did not perform, but was seated in the audience. Celebs in attendance were Sting, Penny Marshall, Twiggy, and Sir George Martin. "Standing Stone" premiere, Royal Albert Hall, London, England, October 14, 1997.

Paul, sans front tooth, sings "Rave On" at his annual Buddy Holly party held at the Roseland Ballroom in New York. "Good evening, New York! How ya doin'? All right? Having a good time? Thanks for coming. As usual, we haven't rehearsed. But it's Okay. Give me an 'A.' *[Sings the note opera style]* Well-a-ell, little things you say and do . . ." In attendance were 2,500 invitation-only guests. Many won tickets through radio stations and the Internet. Celebrities included Christopher Reeve, Gilbert Gottfried, Darlene Love, Neil Sedaka, Mark McGrath (Sugar Ray), Lou Christie, Chubby Checker, Bobby Vee, Dion DiMucci, JoJo Starbuck, and the Crickets (Buddy Holly's band). Buddy Holly's Rock 'N Roller Dance Party, September 7, 1999.

1999 CONCERT DATES

1999 PERFORMANCES March 15: Rock and Roll Hall of Fame Induction, Waldorf Astoria Hotel, New York, New York • April 10: Here, There, and Everywhere Concert for Linda, Royal Albert Hall, London, England • September 7: Buddy Holly's Rock 'N Roller Dance Party, Roseland Ballroom, New York, New York • September 17: PETA Millennium Gala, Paramount Pictures, Hollywood, California • December 14: Cavern, Liverpool, England

ADMIT ONE

MPL
PRESENTS
**Buddy Holly's
Rock 'N Roller Dance
Party 1999**
TUESDAY, SEPTEMBER 7, 1999
ROSELAND BALLROOM
239 WEST 52ND STREET · NEW YORK CITY
8:00 PM – MIDNIGHT

ADMIT ONE

14th ANNUAL
**ROCK AND ROLL
HALL OF FAME®**

INDUCTION
CEREMONY
March 15, 1999

© 1985

PRESS

A proud Paul waves his induction award in the press room. "Hi guys, hi gals. What's happening? *[Reporters shout questions all at once]* What? *[Sings in an Elvis voice]* WEE-ell who's, ma-ool, and sa-aves a life. Sorry!" Fourteenth Annual Rock and Roll Hall of Fame Induction Ceremony, March 15, 1999, Waldorf Astoria Hotel, New York, New York.

Paul and his daughter Stella pose for photos in the press room of the Waldorf Astoria Hotel in New York where the Rock and Roll Hall of Fame Induction ceremony was held. Stella is wearing her controversial T-shirt that reads "ABOUT F*ING TIME!," criticizing the Hall of Fame for not inducting her father when he was eligible several years earlier. At that time Linda was still alive. Paul looks a little disturbed because some male members of the press are calling for Stella. Fourteenth Annual Rock and Roll Hall of Fame Induction Ceremony, March 15, 1999.

Date Due

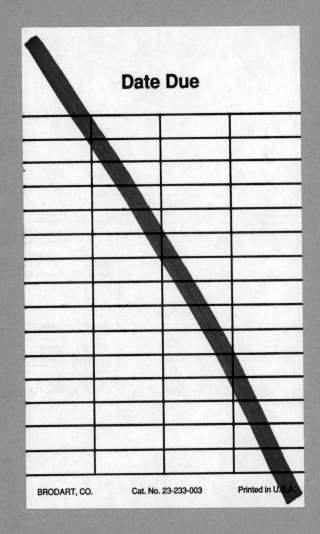

BRODART, CO.　　　Cat. No. 23-233-003　　　Printed in U.S.A.